Also by Donald P. Evans

Still Hooked on Harness Racing
Hanover: The Greatest Name in Harness Racing
Super Bird: The Story of Albatross
Nevele Pride: Speed 'n' Spirit
Big Bum: The Story of Bret Hanover
Hooked on Harness Racing

Rambling
Willie

The Horse that
God Loved

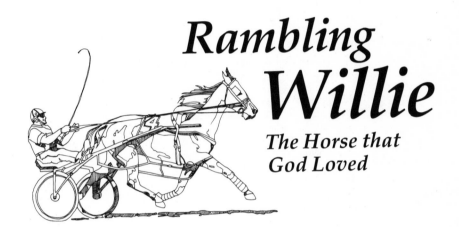

Rambling
Willie

The Horse that God Loved

by Donald P. Evans

and

Philip Pikelny

SAN DIEGO • NEW YORK
A. S. BARNES & COMPANY, INC.
IN LONDON:
THE TANTIVY PRESS

Rambling Willie

The Horse that God Loved copyright ©1981 by Donald P. Evans and Philip Pikelny.

All rights reserved under International and Pan American Copyright Conventions. No part of this book may be reproduced in any manner whatsoever without written permission from the publisher, except in the case of brief quotations embodied in reviews and articles.

First Edition
Manufactured in the United States of America

Verses marked TLB are taken from The Living Bible, copyright 1971 by Tyndale House Publishers, Wheaton, Ill. Used by permission.

For information write to:
A. S. Barnes & Company, Inc.
P.O. Box 3051
La Jolla, California 92038

The Tantivy Press
Magdalen House
136-148 Tooley Street
London, SE1 2TT, England

Library of Congress Cataloging in Publication

Evans, Donald P.
    Rambling Willie: the horse that God loved.

    1. Rambling Willie (Race horse) 2. Farrington, Bob.
3. Farrington, Vivian. 4. Harness racing — United
States. I. Pikelny, Philip S., joint author.
II. Title.
SF343.R35E93   798.4'6   80-26884
ISBN 0-498-02542-X

1   2   3   4   5   6   7   8   9   84   83   82   81

Acknowledgments

While we, the authors, will happily accept whatever glory that happens to sift down from this book, the work would not have been possible without the donation of time and talent by many others. The list includes George Smallsreed, Joe Goldstein, Ed Syguda and Dean Bungart of our own USTA staff, as well as Les Ford of *Harness Horse* magazine and John Berry of the Standardbred Breeders and Owners Association.

Also due a hearty thanks are Jim Curran, Frank Pennino, Walter Paisley, John Miritello, Bob Gordon, Ray Gibson, John Brown, Margaret Hart, Al Bernard and the Chicago *Tribune's* Mike Kiley.

It goes without saying that the Rambling Willie family—Bob and Vivian Farrington, Paul Seibert, Helen Farrington, Steve Rosmarin and Dean Collins—deserve our eternal gratitude.

The inspirational leader of the project, the *force* behind it, was Ken Wales, a Hollywood producer who is easily several hundred cuts above the typical Hollywood producer.

But the largest mandate of our thanks must be reserved for Rambling Willie himself. There has never been another like Willie—and there never will be.

Introduction

Rambling Willie is the real Rocky of our day.
And Rocky II and Rocky III.
He's real, and he's still racing—and still winning!

Every time Willie races these days, he writes a new chapter in his own magnificent story. And every time he wins, he sets a new American record. He's even getting close to being the winningest horse of all time, in the whole world, by any standard!

I learned to love harness racing, and especially the handsome, highly charged horses themselves, while I was making my second movie, *April Love*. I experienced the special communication between a driver and his horse, conveyed through the hands and involving a keen sensitivity—almost like a running conversation—between man and animal, and demanding the best each has to give. The partnership was thrilling, and I quickly developed a deep admiration for the horses and the special qualities that create champions like Rambling Willie.

But the best part, the thing about Willie that makes him so special to all of us, is his *commonness*. Like the fictional Rocky, his credentials are unimpressive. No expert, no wise handicapper, no seasoned horseman would ever have dreamed that Rambling Willie had such "stuff" in him.

He seemed to be "just another horse."
Like you and me.
And he is.

But there's an extra ingredient, and it's impossible to say for sure whether it's inherited or acquired.

It's called heart.
Desire.
Determination.

This quality has lifted Willie out of the ordinary, earned him immortality in racing history. And he thrills me to my socks because he makes me feel that *I* can rise above what might have been expected of *me*.

Rambling Willie's story does that for people.

And then, there's the supernatural. That's part of his story, and you can't explain it away. It's there. It's in the record.

God loves this horse.

And He loves the people who own and race him, the people who've written about him and watched and wondered about him—and the people who've finally had to admit, because of Rambling Willie, that there must be a God who still performs miracles.

I know it's unorthodox.

Lots of "church folks" may be scandalized, as many have been already.

But argue with God. He's the One who has demonstrated, in many unmistakable ways, that He's involved with this horse and his unique story, and in the lives of the people around him.

In the twenty-second chapter of the Bible's Book of Numbers, there's another incredible story about the way God used an ordinary mule to speak to a prophet and a people—in an extraordinary way.

So He's done it before.

And He's doing it again.

I believe the Lord of all creation is surprising us, unsettling us, shocking us, by speaking today through an "ordinary" horse in an extraordinary way.

I won't try to spell out the message, or how it's told, but it comes through loud and clear in this gripping true story of a people's champion—and the champion's people.

Read all about it.

And *go*, Rambling Willie!

Pat Boone
Beverly Hills, California

S*weat* leaked down from Bob Farrington's helmet and ran the length of his face like little rivers as he stood silently near the paddock drawgate at the Sportsman's Park harness racing track some ten miles west of Chicago.

Farrington looked bored. Or, more accurately, sour. He was about to climb into a sulky and drive a horse in a morning qualifying race, a chore he did not relish.

Farrington was a money driver, one of the best. While there was a time when he would have been thrilled to drive any horse in any race at any time, those days had long since passed. Now it griped him to have to put his talent—and his health—on the line in a morning contest that carried no purse. A race designed only to qualify horses for the pari-mutuel races at night.

He felt uneasy, somehow put-upon, although it had been his decision to handle Cheslind, his entry, in the event. Maybe it's the weather, he thought, whipping off his helmet and wiping a hand across his perspiring forehead. Maybe it's just old age coming on, he added.

"Horses on the track for the third race," paddock judge Frank Pennino announced, managing to sound like a rural schoolmaster summoning a bunch of pupils in from recess.

Driver Farrington accepted the horse's lines, slid sideways onto the seat, then swung his short legs around so that they ended up in the stirrups of the sulky.

"Luck, Bob," caretaker Jeff Wright offered in a kind of harness racing ritual.

"May need it with this horse," Farrington responded grimly.

Cheslind was a "green"—inexperienced—pacer, one of forty-nine horses he had bought during a giant equine shopping spree in Australia the past winter. Farrington strongly suspected the pacer was not one of the prize items from the Australian grab bag as he steered him onto the track, where the horse joined five others in a brief limbering-up jog down the stretch before lining up behind the starting gate.

The mobile gate, with one man steering from the driver's seat and a second operating the extended wings from a glass box at the vehicle's rear, collected the horses in front of the grandstand and guided them over to the backside of the track, where it zoomed away, its wings folding, leaving the field scurrying for position.

Cheslind was away in a hurry, although Farrington could see he wasn't likely to wrest the lead away from a speed-crazy pacer that had left from a post position inside him. Contentedly, he moved his horse into the desirable two-spot behind the front-runner. It was the best place to be in a harness race, the so-called "garden spot."

Normally, he would have kept his horse at the heels of the leader to the head of the stretch, then taken off after him in the final eighth of the mile race. But, as the field was nearing the quarter-pole, he noticed Walter "Butch" Paisley ranging up alongside with his horse, Carol Cress. It was obvious that Paisley could not make it to the front with his big, sloppy-gaited pacer and was destined to spend the entire mile "parked out"—blocked from the rail, having to go a longer distance. Since it was only a meaningless qualifying race, Farrington resolved to help his fellow driver, to give him a spot along the rail.

He tugged firmly on Cheslind's lines to slow his horse and was turning to invite Paisley into the hole in front of him when it happened.

Farrington could see the accident unfolding as though it were transpiring in slow motion. But, almost forlornly, he was powerless to prevent it.

Carol Cress, instead of gliding smoothly into the ready-made gap, chose that moment to break stride, leaping out of control, then lurching violently to the right.

"On a break! On a break!" Paisley bellowed as the momentum of his horse's wild dance flung his sulky to the left, sending it smashing into Farrington's bike and buckling the rear legs of Farrington's horse.

Cheslind headed for the unyielding surface of the Sportsman's Park track, the right side of his nine hundred-pound body fated to bear the brunt of the collision. Halfway through the horse's fall, Farrington was catapulted out of the sulky, his compact frame sailing almost gracefully over the rump of the falling pacer. His right shoulder and head struck the turf about the time that Cheslind was landing in a heavy heap behind him.

The force of the unplanned dive sent the driver skidding along the turf, plowing a shallow furrow in the topsoil like a base stealer sliding into second base.

Then he slammed into the hubrail.

Amazingly, Farrington was on his feet within seconds, spitting viciously to clear his mouth of the soil it had collected in the slide. He was dazed, but already straining to get his bearings.

The rest of the horses in the race, he sensed, had avoided the spill and were pacing away some one hundred and fifty yards down the track. Paisley and his horse had gone down, too, but both were on their feet, Paisley already yelling for assistance. Out of the corner of his eye Farrington could see at least a dozen people springing into action, fellow trainers and grooms rushing to help him and the heaving, thrashing horse trapped in a tangle of harness, hopples and sulky.

Thank God, I'm out of the woods, he thought triumphantly. But no sooner had that comforting message registered on his brain than the first wave of pain arrived to chase it away. It started in his shoulder, spread across his chest, then settled in his stomach, where it quickly turned to nausea.

"Damn!" he muttered savagely, aware at the moment that he had rebroken his collarbone.

Involuntarily, Farrington hunched forward—like an old, old man—and his left hand shot up to protectively cup the point of his right shoulder.

"You all right, Bob?" asked a young, blond caretaker, the first of the breathless rescuers to reach him. The young man, whom Farrington knew by sight but not name, had won the foot race to the driver, but was ignorant of what to do with his victory. He reached up and pulled Farrington's red and gray driver's silks, which were caught up around his chest. Then he began to brush dirt from the silks.

"Easy!" Farrington yelped, shrinking from the youngster's eager hands.

"Sorry, Bob. Sorry," the teen-ager apologized.

"Pin the horse," Farrington directed.

"Do what?"

"Pin the horse. Sit on his head. Keep him still."

By this time, others were arriving—Pennino, the paddock judge, Nick Colini, the driver of the starting gate, and a flock of horsemen who had been watching the morning qualifiers from the drawgate.

Experienced hands were stripping the struggling horse of its equipment. The youngster and an older man were sprawled across Cheslind's neck and head, using leverage to keep him down while the tack was removed. And Bob Farrington, pain and all, was directing traffic.

"Watch it," he cautioned. "The field's coming."

The mishap had occurred a few yards beyond the quarter-pole, where the first—and final—curve of the egg-shaped, five-eighths mile track began to straighten into the stretch. The four surviving horses in the contest had circled the oval and were bearing down on the accident scene.

Quickly, the small band of Farrington saviors fled to the outside fence, the barrier between the track and the grandstand apron. The two men pinning Cheslind's head held their ground, but watched warily as the field swept past, the alert drivers giving the scene wide berth.

One horse, frightened by the motley collection of man and animal on both sides of the track, jumped in the air, but landed safely and galloped awkwardly down the stretch.

Walter Paisley, with his horse safely in other hands, joined the collection as Farrington's pacer, now naked of his racing gear, scrambled to his feet. Petrified, Cheslind gasped for breath, but was otherwise unhurt. Paisley paid the horse no heed.

Panting, with streams of sweat mingling with dust from the track on his face, he rushed up to Farrington. "Man, I'm sorry, Bob. Sick about it. Believe me, that damn skin of mine jumped it off without a bit of warning. No warning at all. No reason. . . ."

Paisley, looking younger than his thirty-one years, was suffering. His boyish, freckle-dotted face was wrinkled with concern. He seemed close to tears. Bob Farrington was his friend. Farrington had always helped him. Had helped him grab a foothold in the rough and tough, closed circle that was the Chicago harness racing arena in the early 1960s. Had given him horses to drive, good horses, when the older driver was sidelined by injury, illness or suspension. Farrington, in fact, was doing him another favor—giving him a spot along the rail—when he and his miserable, misbehaving pacing mare had put him on the ground.

"Not your fault," Bob replied somberly. The shoulder was now hurting like a giant toothache, streaks of pain shooting out at ever more frequent intervals.

"You hurt bad?" Paisley demanded, fearing, knowing the answer.

"Shoulder," Farrington said dully.

"Same one?"

"Yeah."

"Damn," Paisley murmured, then added loudly, "Somebody call the track ambulance. Get the ambulance. This man's hurt!"

"Way ahead of you, Butch," somebody offered dryly. "In fact, it's about to knock you on your can."

With that, the ambulance, an efficient looking, yellow Buick leased by the track to handle emergencies at both the nighttime pari-mutuel races and the morning qualifying contests, skidded to a stop. Two attendants popped out. The first took a quick glance at Farrington, saw a short, slender, yet powerfully built man, bent at the waist with pain, and yelled to his partner, "Get the stretcher."

"No stretcher," Farrington growled.

"You better," the attendant advised.

"No. Leave under my own power. I'll sit in front," he said, gingerly slipping onto the seat, the left hand offering support to the fractured clavicle.

Paisley, still stricken, stuck his head in the open window. "Damn, Bob, what can I say? Damn, damn, damn. What a helluva thing. Geez, I'm sorry. Real sorry. What can I do to help? Whataya need. . . ."

"See that somebody calls Vivian," Farrington said weakly as the ambulance pulled away, its rear wheels creating little spouts of flying dirt.

"It'll get done, Bob. Don't worry, we'll call her. And I'm sorry. . . ." Paisley aimed at the departing vehicle.

The ambulance shot down the stretch, headed for the stable area exit onto Laramie Avenue. Bob Farrington, with the awful ache carving even deeper lines in his normally craggy face, stared gloomily out the window. The Sportsman's Park grandstand, now empty and cavernous in the light of day, seemed to mock him as the Buick flew by.

It was Tuesday, July 11, 1972, an awesomely hot and humid day, and Bob Farrington had been training and driving harness horses professionally for seventeen years when Paisley's horse sent him crashing to the earth.

They had been good years, no question about that. But they had been rugged years, too. And with his throbbing collarbone acting as a catalyst, Farrington did not have to rummage long in his memory to recall the parade of serious injuries he'd suffered along the way.

The right shoulder had been shattered the first time in a pile-up at Maywood Park, Maywood, Illinois, in 1967. Five ribs were broken in the same spill.

Three years later, racing at Washington Park, a busy track on the south side of Chicago, he'd been dumped out of the sulky into the middle of a large race field, with the trailing horses kicking and trampling him into unconsciousness. The big crowd of fans looking on thought he was dead, but he had escaped with broken cheekbones on both sides of his face, a fractured nose, severe facial cuts, and bruises from one end of his body to the other.

His longest vacation from the track had started on New Year's Day of 1968, when he'd emerged from a multi-horse tumble at Bay Meadows, outside of San Francisco, with a broken leg. He had tried to walk away from that one, but the leg had collapsed, giving him three months to catch up on his reading and television game shows.

An accident at Windsor Raceway, Windsor, Canada, had merely ripped cartilage loose from several ribs, plus severely bruised—but not broken—the same shoulder he was nursing now.

"Man," he said aloud, breaking the silence in the ambulance as it hastened along 31st Street, lights flashing but no siren wailing, making good time in the sparse, pre-noontime traffic.

"Huh?" said the startled driver.

"Nothing really. I was just thinking . . . I could have been killed out there. A guy my age driving a cheap horse in a worthless qualifying race. I got to be nuts."

"How old are you, Bob?"

"Be forty-three on Saturday."

"Hell, that's not old," the medic in the back of the Buick contributed cheerfully.

"It is in this game. It sure is in this game," Farrington declared, his voice trailing off.

And it was. Sure, Frank Ervin had raced horses until he was pushing seventy; hadn't started to campaign world champion Bret Hanover until he'd turned sixty, as a matter of fact. And Earle Avery and Sanders Russell, two more big names in the harness sport? Why, they were both approaching eighty before they'd climbed down from the bike. But those guys were the exception, not the rule. Those guys had campaigned on the Grand Circuit, the major league of racing, where they only raced seven or eight times a week. Give them fifty or sixty horses, plant them at a raceway to stay, and how long would they have lasted?

A raceway driver settling in at one track or town, skilled and in demand, was called upon to go to post eight hundred, a thousand, even twelve hundred times a year. That's what took it out of you, made you old before your time—racing horses six, seven, or eight times *a night.* That kind of grind was tailored for the young—for Walt Paisley, Jim Curran, young bucks like that. Not for some beat-up, leathery-faced codger about to turn forty-three, Farrington mused ruefully.

"Almost there, Bob," the ambulance driver offered. "We're on Ogden now, coming into Berwyn. Flip a right on Oak Park and you'll find Mac Neal Hospital on your right."

"The sooner, the better. I need some help." Farrington could feel the heat and the swelling in his shoulder, the big and ugly knob forming. And he knew exactly what it would look like when they pulled off his racing silks and cut away his

T-shirt. He'd been there before.

What would it be this time? he wondered. The gloomy guys in the funny white uniforms and masks digging around in there with the sharp little instruments, planting a pin here, a pin there? Or would it be traction, with a flock of folks full of false cheer assembling to set and lock his arm into a kind of grotesque Hitler salute, the arm to remain in that position until Hell started to freeze over?

Was it time to pack it in? he asked himself. Time to hang up the scarlet and gray silks and turn the driving over to those young bucks?

By God, maybe it was!

Lloyd Arnold, his stable partner, had been urging him to do just that, had been prodding him to concentrate on training and on locating new horses to add to the stable. Jim Curran, Bob's son-in-law, had been driving some of the stable's horses, and doing well at it, too. Couldn't Curran handle all of them?

And winding down his driving career, wouldn't that simplify his racing operation, maybe get the Internal Revenue Service, which always seemed to challenge his return, off his back?

And those few but vociferous fans who insisted that he cheated with his horses—why was it they only picked on the successful drivers?—wouldn't they give him some peace if he were not around so much; not so public, not so visible?

And most important of all, must he go on climbing into sulkies, steering trotters and pacers in and out of tight holes and situations at thirty miles an hour until disaster struck yet again and he was permanently crippled or killed?

Robert G. Farrington arrived at his decision as the Buick ambulance was pulling up to the emergency entrance of the community-run hospital.

He was out of the car, through the double doors, walking up the ramp with an attendant at each side as though they were escorting a drunk, and a harried-looking nurse was saying, "We're very busy and we're going to have to bed him down in the hallway for the time being."

Farrington hardly heard. He was wondering how Vivian would take the news that the glory days were over.

Chapter 2

*V*ivian Farrington, wife of harness racing driver Bob Farrington, was puttering about the couple's twentieth-floor apartment in fashionable Lake Point Towers, along Chicago's Lake Shore Drive. Flicking a dust rag here, flicking it there.

Nothing truly needed her attention. The roomy, modern, luxurious apartment with off-white walls and thick, plum-hued, shag carpeting seemed to take care of itself. It had, in fact, an almost antiseptic look about it. She and Bob simply did not spend enough time there to provide the subtle clutter so necessary in lending a lived-in feel to a home.

Yet, it gave her pleasure to wander about the rooms, straightening this, dusting that. She did it every day, paying particular attention to the trophy case. On its shelves were silver, gold, glass and pewter mementos of some of the important races Bob had won, of some of the national honors he had received. The lesser awards were back at their farm in Richwood, Ohio. Scores of them.

She was admiring them now, the metal and crystal reminders of great victories scored, when the phone rang.

Unconsciously, she folded the dust rag, laid it neatly on the arm of an overstuffed chair, and tugged at her skirt to remove wrinkles that were not present before picking up the receiver.

"Hello," she said, her voice soft, well modulated.

"Vivian?"

"Yes."

"Phil Langley."

"Phil? Is something wrong?" She had been married to a harness horse trainer-driver long enough to know that racing secretaries were not in the habit of phoning a horseman's home when the horseman was there at the secretary's track training horses. And Phil Langley was the racing secretary at Sportsman's Park, where Bob was headed when he had left the apartment at 7:30 that morning.

"Now don't panic, Vivian. But there was an accident in a qualifying race here this morning. . . ."

"Bob?"

"Bob."

"And he's hurt. How badly?"

"Nobody knows yet; he was taken to Mac Neal Hospital over in Berwyn for x-rays. But I can assure you, he was up, walking around, talking. So it doesn't look that bad . . . that serious, all things considered."

Somehow Langley's voice fell somewhat short of matching the confidence contained in his words.

"Where was he hurt? What has to be x-rayed?"

"I'm not sure. Looked like it might be his arm. Maybe his shoulder."

"His right shoulder?"

"Viv, I can't remember. Could have been."

"Not again," Mrs. Farrington murmured.

"Might have been his left," Langley interjected quickly.

"No. No, with his luck, I'm sure it was the right; the one he broke so badly at Washington Park, then reinjured at Windsor."

"Listen, Viv. Do you have a way to get over to the hospital? Shall I send a car for you?"

"No. Oh, no, that won't be necessary. There's a taxi stand right out in front of the building."

"You're sure?"

"Positive. And Phil, thanks for calling. I know it's not easy. . . ."

"It sure as hell isn't."

Vivian Farrington placed the receiver back in the cradle and gracefully dropped to her knees. Kneeling, she began to pray. There was no sense of the dramatic about her action, no aura of a role being played. For Vivian Farrington, it was a natural thing to do, a normal response to crisis.

Since earliest childhood she had been taught to thank God for His kindnesses. And to seek His help in times of need. In Vivian's mind, God had never failed her. And wouldn't this time.

In a matter of minutes, she was on her feet, calmly gathering the items—toothbrush, razor, shaving cream, pajamas, cigarettes—her husband would need if he were to remain in the hospital. She filled the small overnight bag, grabbed her purse, and started for the door.

She paused as she reached the telephone, but resisted the urge to call their daughter, Karen; she'd do it from the hospital. Automatically, she glanced at the mirror above the telephone stand. A pretty face, framed by short, straw-colored hair, stared back at her. And the face had the look of serenity, of tranquility. Faith had put it there.

Down on the street, with the mod-shaped structure behind her and shimmering Lake Michigan off to her right, she waited for a cab. It was noon now, and the sun, high in the sky, was sending down robust rays that bounced off the Chicago streets, creating ghostly waves of energy that hovered a few inches above their surface. She gazed at the lake, envying the distant figures who tinkered with the tillers of a profusion of sailboats sprinkled over the water.

Vivian was relieved to feel the rush of cool air as she slid onto the seat of the air conditioned taxi.

"Where to, lady?"

The voice was the property of a slightly built man of Italian or maybe Greek extraction. His head was perilously short of hair, and his cheeks could have used a quick shave that morning. But a pleasant smile was firmly in place upon his face.

"Do you think you can find Mac Neal Hospital over in Berwyn?" Mrs. Farrington asked.

"Find it? Of course I can find it," he shot back, as though his competence had been questioned. But then he added solicitously, "Somebody sick in the family?"

"No. There's been an accident."

"Geez, I'm sorry," the driver offered, pressing a little harder on the accelerator. "Someone hurt bad?"

"I don't know. I don't think so. At least I hope not. It's my husband."

"I'm sorry," he repeated. "But I can't say I'm surprised.

These Chicago streets, they get worse every day. More crowded. More dangerous. Fulla people who don't know how to drive. Who knows better than me?"

Vivian would have preferred to ride in silence. To use the time for meditation, for thought, for more prayer. But she sensed the slender cabbie was going to provide little time for any of that.

"It wasn't a car crash. My husband's a harness racing driver. He was hurt in a qualifying race at Sportsman's Park this morning."

"Oh, yeah? Who's your husband?" the driver asked with new interest.

"Bob Farrington," she responded softly.

"The Red Man?"

"Yes," Vivian answered, smiling in spite of herself. To harness racing fans throughout the Chicago area, where Bob Farrington had concentrated his racing for a dozen years, Bob was the "Red Man." It had nothing to do with the color of his skin, but rather with the scarlet of his racing colors.

"You the Red Man's wife?" he demanded, both surprised and delighted.

"Yes. I'm Vivian Farrington."

"Well, whataya know, the Red Man's wife! How about that!

"Mrs. Farrington . . . Vivian . . . I'm Vito Colucci, probably the greatest fan your husband's got in this world. I've made thousands betting him over the years. Thousands, I tell ya. At Sportsman's, at Washington Park, at Maywood, at all the Chicago tracks. He's the greatest harness driver in the world, bar none."

Certainly *among* the greatest in the world, Vivian thought. The first driver in history to score two hundred wins in a season. The first to score three hundred. The national dash-winning champion for six out of seven years in the 1960s. A career winner of more than 2,800 races and nearly $7 million in racing purses. The perennial local champion at all the Chicago tracks, plus a number of them in California, New York and other states.

Indeed, quite a record for a farm boy out of Ohio, she mused as Colucci continued to chatter away. Married at eighteen. Farming it for a while, then going into construction work, where he'd earned $3.50 an hour as a mason. Laying bricks all day, then training horses in the evening. Finally going with the horses full-time in 1955, touring the Ohio fairs and winding up with a little more than $3,000 in purses, which he'd had to share with his brother, Richard. Hanging in there. Embarrassed that his wife had to hold down two jobs to make ends meet. Living out of a tackroom at some decrepit fairground, sometimes with his wife and young daughter sharing the quarters. Hanging in there. Eventually buying a small house trailer when things began to improve. Having a fine year in Ohio in 1959, then moving on to the big time—Chicago—where his explosive driving style put his career in orbit. . . .

"Geez, the Red Man hurt again," Vito Colucci was saying with feeling, interrupting her reverie. "What a shame. What a damn shame!"

Vivian, lost in her thoughts and trapped into listening to the driver, had not realized how far they had traveled. The bustle of downtown Chicago was behind them. So were the freeways. So were the industrial plants and the warehouses, as a matter of fact. Colucci, swiftly, but with the smoothness of a professional, was steering the checkered vehicle along suburban streets, timing streetlights perfectly, spending only an instant at stop signs.

The cab driver grew mellow. Then preachy. "I'll tell ya, Vivian, guys like me who've been plunging on Bob for years know darn well he's straight, that he gives us an honest shake every crack out of the box. But we worry about him when we read that some unidentified hood has threatened him, has left some crummy note somewhere that says he's gonna get hurt if he don't cooperate with the crooks. And he's got to be more careful about these accidents, too. I mean he could end up a helpless. . . ."

"I know," Vivian said from the back seat. "I know."

"That was the wrong thing to say," Vito added hastily. "I was way out of line. . . ."

"What you said was true. There's no need to apologize."

". . . But I'm an optimist," the driver continued. "And I'm hoping you find he's okay this time. Maybe some bumps and bruises, that kind of thing. And you're gonna know soon, 'cause here's the hospital."

Vivian looked up to see a two-wing complex connected by

a main entrance. The hospital, built of beige bricks, was neither large nor small, neither new nor old. It faced busy Oak Park Avenue, while drowsy, tree-lined Euclid Avenue was at its rear.

"What entrance do you want, Mrs. Farrington?" inquired the cabbie, suddenly turning formal, the intimidating hospital reminding him of the seriousness of his mission.

"The emergency, I'd say," she responded.

"Sure," said Colucci.

In a couple of minutes he had homed in on the back entrance, and Vivian was climbing out of the car, eyeing an ambulance ramp to her right and a door to her left.

"Thanks, Mrs. Farrington," the driver offered as he accepted her fare. Then, as she was turning to begin the short walk to the door, he added shyly, haltingly, "Say, Vivian . . . I know he's gonna be fine. But even so, tell the Red Man . . . tell the Red Man . . . that Vito Colucci's gonna say a little prayer for him, will ya? Whatever that's worth. . . ."

"It's worth a lot, Vito. Believe me, it all helps." Then she turned and entered the door.

Inside, everything was pretty much as it was an hour earlier when Bob had arrived. Vivian negotiated the enclosed ramp and arrived at a long corridor with rooms jutting off from both sides. The harried-looking nurse was still there, but this time standing at a nursing station, busy with some sort of complicated-looking form. With surprise, she spotted her husband stretched out on a narrow, wheeled cot or bed, some fifteen or twenty feet up the hallway. She resisted the urge to rush to him. Instead, she stopped dutifully at the nurse's window and identified herself.

"He's right up there," the nurse said, voicing the obvious and compounding it by pointing at the prone horseman. "We haven't done much with him yet. Still waiting to get him down to x-ray."

"Can I see him?" Vivian inquired.

"By all means. I suspect he'll be glad to see *someone.* Heaven knows he hasn't seen many of us, the way this madhouse has been going today. I think everybody in the county waited to get sick or hurt on July 11."

While the corridor was reasonably free of people, Vivian

could sense a great deal of activity going on behind the closed doors. Occasionally, a white-clad nurse or intern would hustle in or out of the doors, a solemn or determined expression on each face. She could hear the screams of a child from one of the rooms.

Bob was flat on his back, his head toward her as she approached, so he was unaware of her presence until she arrived at the foot of his small bed. She was gratified to see the light snap on in his eyes as he focused on her, but distressed to notice that it was his left arm that shot up so that he could grasp her outstretched hand. That meant the injury was to the right shoulder, the one that had been injured so severely in the past.

He seemed a study in contrasts as she looked down at him. His face was tan and leathery, like a farmer's, from the thousands of hours of riding in a jog cart. His chest, she knew, was overdeveloped, like a weight lifter's, from tugging at the lines attached to stubborn horses. And the muscles in the arm that reached up to hold her hand were huge, like those on the hitting arm of a professional tennis player.

Yet, in seeing him now, his face seemed wan, drawn, rather gray against the white of the pillow. His body, for all the power from his waist up, looked small, almost fragile, as it rested on the hospital mattress.

"Got a lot of pain, Honey?" she asked.

"Not bad," he said, always the Spartan. "They gave me a pill a while ago."

"The right shoulder?"

"Yeah."

"Oh, Bob," she said, her eyes misting.

"C'mon, Viv. None of that."

"Bob, is this going to happen again and again."

He was silent for a moment. "Nooo . . ." he answered slowly. "No, it's not."

"What's that mean?" she pressed.

"Viv, we'll talk about it later. When they get me out of this thoroughfare and into a room. Did you call Karen?"

"I haven't. I came directly here after Phil Langley called."

"You better call her. And while you're at it, ask Florence Nightingale down there if I can have a drink of water and a cigarette."

Vivian was back in five minutes. "Karen is on her way. But the nurse says no water or cigarettes. Something about x-rays."

Farrington groaned.

Hours passed before the trainer was removed from the corridor, x-rayed, and assigned to a room. But they were broken up by the arrival of several anxious visitors—Rita Zeinfeld and Adele Vollaro, wives of Chicago area horsemen; the Farringtons' daughter, Karen, the small, pretty wife of young harness driver Jim Curran; and Walter Paisley, still wearing a cloak of self-inflicted guilt from the morning wreck, apparently seeking further absolution from victim Farrington.

"You got nothing to feel guilty about," Farrington told him flatly, though Paisley would continue to be an almost daily visitor throughout his friend's hospital stay.

Vivian was alone with him when the doctor finally arrived to explain his options. The physician, tall, stern-looking, with a bristly, gray crewcut, pointed out that Bob's right clavicle, as suspected, was fractured, and in the same spot where it had been broken earlier. And just as Farrington had feared, the menu contained but two main courses: surgery or traction.

"Traction," said the harness driver.

"At least four weeks, maybe five," counseled the doctor.

"Traction," said Farrington.

"We don't offer guarantees with these things," the doctor warned. "They can be tricky. Don't always heal just the way you want them to."

"Traction."

"Traction it is," the doctor agreed.

Vivian Farrington remained silent throughout the exchange. She had always permitted her man to make the big decisions—what he would do for a living, where they would live, where he would race, and, in the old days, what horse they would buy with their meager life savings.

But there was one decision, a crucial one, that she wished mightily he would surrender to her. She had prayed for that power, for that important proxy, in the living room of their apartment before leaving for the hospital.

Then, suddenly, she had no need of it.

"Viv," Bob was saying, "I don't know how you're going to

take this, but I've pretty well made up my mind to quit driving racehorses. . . ."

Vivian stared at him.

". . . Or quit driving at the raceways, at least. Maybe just enough to keep my finger in the game, enough to keep my license alive.

"Honey, I'm sick to death of laying in these lousy hospital beds. I'm sick of rushing out to this track or that track night after night. I'm weary of climbing off one sulky and hopping onto the next. And I'm weary of hearing the fans curse at me when I get beat with a favorite. But most of all, I'm tired of worrying about the next accident, wondering if that'll be the one that makes a gimp out of me. . . ."

She continued to gaze at him, but the tears were marring her vision.

"Honey, I understand you're going to miss it," he continued. "The excitement. The travel. The awards. The. . . ."

"Thank you, Lord," Vivian announced gently.

"What? What'd you say, Viv?"

"I was thanking the Lord."

"The Lord? What are you thanking the Lord for?" Bob demanded.

"For guiding you to that judgment."

"The *Lord*? What's He got to do with it? It wasn't Him; it was that damn fool pacing mare of Paisley's. She's the one that made up my mind for me."

Vivian shook her head slowly. Then she brushed the tears from her eyes and leaned over to kiss her husband.

Chapter 3

*M*r. Harris . . . it's already past four. You oughta get going!"

The words struck more of an entreaty than an exhortation. The voice obviously did not enjoy making demands of Clinton Lloyd Harris. It belonged to Jim Goodwin.

At twenty-six, Goodwin adroitly managed his parents' J and J Market. He had a baby face, but that feature never gave anyone cause to doubt his ability or authority to make the emporium run. The store was no supermarket, to be sure, but its four aisles of product-filled shelves, expansive meat counter and assorted sundries certainly kept it from being termed small. It was the only food shop serving the six hundred citizens of Rushsylvania, Ohio. Its size required the control of a man not afraid to make decisions.

Yet, despite his talents and his birthright, Goodwin never felt comfortable when it came to directing the employee who was fifty-four years his senior.

Goodwin's discomfort did not arise from Harris' demeanor or age. Despite his eighty years, Harris' body was unusually supple, strong and steady. His face was kindly, usually sporting a smile. His manner was deferential, gentle.

Goodwin simply figured that his elder never needed much direction. Harris was the hardest worker at the rustic market, and had been for years. Area teen-agers arrived and disappeared from Goodwin's payroll so fast, some could hardly be distinguished from customers. Oblivious to the turnover, the oldster labored on. When something had to be moved, lifted, marked, parked, checked, cut, delivered, or bagged, Harris—

the old fellow with the body and will that totally belied his age—was always first to the job.

Most men of eighty would be content to pass their remaining time plucking catfish from a river. Others might prefer to lull themselves to sleep by rocking in a chair. Just a few days earlier, Harris was climbing ladders to rehabilitate the old store's roof. At present, he was trimming the fat from a section of beef sirloin, portioning off a steak large enough to feed a family of four.

"Please, Mr. Harris," implored the fretting young boss, "you know you've got to leave early. I'll wrap the meat."

Harris was grinning as Goodwin's young hands encased the blood-red beef in waxed white paper. He should have been on his way out the door, but he hated to leave a chore half done. Sort of old-fashioned, maybe, but it was his way.

He headed for the front door, but paused near the register. He watched as a young girl, newly employed, haltingly rang up an order. He might have been tempted to assist the novice cashier bag some of the groceries stacked haphazardly between her and an increasingly impatient shopper had not the watchful Goodwin beseeched, *"Please*, get outta here!"

Harris waved a hand in surrender, then exited onto the single block of businesses that was downtown Rushsylvania. The grocery store was at the end of the block. Directly across the street was a bank. There was also a post office. A hardware shop. And a few other assorted establishments.

The sky was cloudy, the weather hot and muggy. Harris spent a glance at the sleepy center of town, then promptly headed up Euclid Street. He was advancing toward the first of a number of appointments, slightly behind schedule.

Euclid Street ran perpendicular to the avenue of downtown stores. It was like all the rest of the residential streets in the tiny town—neat lines of two-storied, wood-framed houses on both sides of the road, each with small patches of grass all around. Closer to the curbs were strings of large maple trees. Harris half-trotted between the rows of trees and homes that made up Euclid. He admired its peacefulness as he made his way toward the house at the end of the block.

Harris was tall and willowy, but like the maple trees to his left, a trifle bent with age. As he came upon the final house, he turned and headed up the walk. There was a lilt in his stride and enthusiasm shining from his face.

He reached the front door and rang the doorbell. A moment later, a woman in her early twenties came in response.

"Good afternoon, young lady," Harris said by way of greeting. "I'm Reverend C. L. Harris. I preach at the Church of Christ over in West Mansfield."

He watched as a measure of surprise flashed across the woman's face. "I read in our local paper," he explained, "that you and your husband are new in town, and I make a practice of welcoming all the new arrivals."

"How thoughtful," she beamed. "You know, you're the first visitor we've had. But I have to tell you, we're Catholic, and not. . . ."

"Oh, I'm not recruiting today," he interrupted politely. Then his face broke into a grandfatherly smile as he added, "I just stopped by to say Hi. You'll find most of the folks around here to be friendly."

Harris continued to talk about Rushsylvania and himself. He answered all of the young woman's questions about her new community, even where she would find the nearest Catholic church.

"I really think we're going to like this town," the woman remarked, smiling. "I just wish my husband were here to meet you."

"I'd like that, too," Harris agreed. "But right now, I'd best be on my way. Got a lot of errands to run today." He began to turn from the door to leave, when he decided to add, "Just because you're not in my church, don't think we can't be friends. You're both welcome to visit, any time. Bonny, that's my wife, and I only live two blocks up the street. We're the first house on the left, after you pass the stop sign at the center of town. The white one.

"Don't be strangers," he concluded.

Reverend Harris enjoyed making these calls. They were among the things he liked best about being a minister. In the fifty years since he had graduated from the Johnson Bible College near Knoxville, Tennessee, he had married more than eleven hundred couples and buried more than twenty-two hundred folks. He had baptized hundreds of people and delivered thousands of sermons. Still, meeting new neighbors seemed to be among the more satisfying tasks he performed.

Harris knew how important a social visit by a minister could be to new folks in town. He remembered the days when he had left his hometown of West Plains, Missouri. He was late into his teens when he went in search of the generous wages being paid to boys his age who would work the farmlands in the northeastern part of Iowa.

Harris settled in the city of Greene. He was alone for the first time in his life. Over five hundred and fifty miles separated the youth from his family—a father, stepmother, and an aunt who had raised him in his early years after his natural mother had succumbed of "congestive chills."

Reverend Roy Crocker was the minister at the local Church of Christ in Greene. Late in the summer, the clergyman invited the lad to his home. Harris welcomed the opportunity to share the company and conversation of the jovial preacher.

C. L. Harris never fashioned himself to be particularly religious. He had been baptized as a child and was regularly attending Crocker's church on Sundays since arriving at the new town, but that was where it ended. He was dumbfounded at the pastor's suggestion that night over dinner, recommending he join the ministry. It was the last thing he had planned to do with his life.

But Crocker understood the workings of Harris' mind. "You can get a free education at the Johnson Bible College," he explained. "Boys go in rags, with no money, and work off their tuition while attending school and during summer vacations."

It wasn't much later that Harris and a friend, Morris Wieneke, boarded a train bound for the Tennessee college. Once the transportation was paid for, Harris had ten dollars left to his name. It was just enough to cover his admission.

Wieneke didn't last two weeks, homesick for the familiar plains and farmlands of Iowa. Crushed by his friend's defection, Harris, too, longed to abandon the campus, but lacked the money to finance the trip. Instead, he persevered. He completed one semester, then a second. . . .

One night during his sophomore year at Johnson, kneeling in prayer, he admitted he had still not made up his mind whether or not to devote his life to the ministry. He looked to the Lord for direction. He thought he heard a voice advise,

"You know what I want you to do." While the ambiguous message failed to supply him with the instant wisdom he sought, it wasn't long before he resolved to commit his future to the service of God.

As he increased his education in the ministry, he received his first experiences as a clergyman through summer pulpit duty at a Central New York church and a part-time preaching position in Knoxville, Tennessee, while still in school.

When he applied for the part-time work in Knoxville, he met his wife-to-be, Bonny Hartsell. Her baptism was one of the rites performed on the day he visited the church. They were married in 1923, and he was ordained a year later.

Harris' first calling was to serve two Ohio congregations—Bluffton and Beaverdam. After only a few months, he transferred to another small Ohio church in Rushsylvania, where he and his wife bought a home and raised a family. Through 1972, he had served five congregations within a thirty-mile radius of his home.

To supplement his preacher's wages and sustain his family—a wife and five children—during much of this half-century of ministration, Harris also held secular jobs. He began at the food mart in Rushsylvania during the Depression years. In 1948, he traded his storekeeper's white smock for the dark pinstripes of a bank teller. The pay was higher, the working conditions better suited to a man of the cloth, and the working agreement between employer and employee remained the same—marriages, baptisms, and death took precedence over loans, deposits and withdrawals. He continued at the bank until 1955, when the Mt. Victory, Ohio, Church of Christ, which he had already served for twenty years, built Harris and his helpmate a parsonage so they could truly serve the congregation on a full-time basis.

Five years later, Harris began to experience his first discomfiture in working for the Lord. He was noticing that many of the young children he had baptized during his first few years at the church were now the parents of children he was christening. Joseph Fittro and Richard Davis, two young lads when Harris began at the church, had entered the ministry and now had their own parishes.

He perceived his effectiveness to the church beginning to wane. He felt more like the parishioners' grandfather than their minister. An injection of new blood was his prescription for the pulpit. He resigned from the Mt. Victory church after a quarter of a century of service and headed home to Rushsylvania.

Retirement was in his mind but not his heart as he settled back into the old house on Euclid Street. He had always planned to preach as long as the Lord permitted, and the Lord had given no indication He was ready to put Harris on the shelf.

Two weeks into retirement, Harris' schedule was as busy as ever. He was called back into the ministry at the Uniopolis Christian Church. He also signed up for three days a week work at the Goodwin's J and J Market, the same store that had hired him thirty years earlier.

Until this hot, humid day in 1972, he had been out of retirement for more than a decade. Nine of those years had been as the minister at the Church of Christ in West Mansfield, located about nine miles southeast of Rushsylvania. If he were going to celebrate his tenth anniversary at the little church, he thought as he started the engine of his green Chevy Impala, he had better make haste to his second appointment of the day.

He had a twenty-five minute drive down country roads to a farm a few miles southwest of the city of West Mansfield, to the home of the George Ackley family. This call would not be as pleasant as the previous visit to his new neighbor had been. Not pleasant at all. George Ackley had died the night before.

The front door of the house was open. Harris entered and quietly approached the widow. He remembered her smile which had been such an inspiration to him and his Sunday worshipers. Now her eyes were red and moist. The expression on her face indicated the depression and grief she was feeling.

She and the reverend shared a few memories. He quoted some Scripture. She shed a few tears. Holding the widow's right hand, Harris reminded her, "All things work together for good to them that love God. Blessed are they that mourn; for they shall be comforted."

A labored, but faint smile of consolation came to the woman's face. It was what he wanted to see. Now that he did, he left.

The time was approaching 6:00 P.M. as Harris completed his drive back to Rushsylvania and parked his auto in front of his house. He hoped to get some rest in his overstuffed recliner before he headed for his church in West Mansfield. He would need the respite since he was scheduled for a wedding rehearsal at 8:00 P.M.

All wedding rehearsals seemed to come complete with a collection of well-meaning mothers, aunts, grandmothers and friends, all self-professed experts on weddings. No matter what directions he gave the bride and groom, there was always a better way. Usually, their way.

Rehearsals probably weren't as bad as he seemed to remember them, but at eighty years of age, trying to appease so many women with differing tastes no longer appealed to him. It never really had.

Following the rehearsal, Harris had promised to meet with the church board to discuss repairs to the old church building. The deacons were worried the treasury could not afford the work that needed to be done. Though the congregation had always managed to meet its obligations in the past, the reverend had to admit that the coming year looked gloomy at best. The aging roof, the worn carpeting, the broken pews and the other items in disrepair inspired that gloom.

Harris wondered whether his meeting with the church's deacons and elders would be the right time to bring up the matter of the new bulletin board he hoped to buy for the exterior of the church. Since he had first seen it at a minister's convention earlier in the year, he knew such a board was unequaled anywhere in Central Ohio. It stood waist high, and would be positioned on the lawn in front of the church. At night, the entire sign lit up.

There was a certain class to the bulletin board, but its $650 price tag also made it a luxury. Knowing the financial state of affairs at his church, Harris decided to shelve his idea until a later date. Maybe forever.

Harris climbed the steps to his home and entered the enclosed front porch that he used as a small office and sitting room during the summer months. "Mother, I'm home," he shouted to let his wife know he had arrived. He didn't expect an answer. They both knew it was his custom to check the mail she had tucked into his antique roll-top desk earlier in the afternoon.

As he leaned back into his swivel chair that serviced an old, wooden roll-top desk, he found a letter he had been anticipating. It was written by one of Harris' former parishioners at Uniopolis, a man in his thirties who had moved his family to the nearby metropolis of Columbus to try a new business venture.

The fellow had taken his savings and invested them in a movie theater located on the border of a small college campus. He was a single scene from bankruptcy when he had contacted his old friend and reverend for counsel two months ago. Harris hoped he had done the young man some good.

His advice was always the same for matters of this type. It came from Malachi, one of the last prophets mentioned in the Old Testament. Malachi preached to a world—sometime around 450 B.C.—confronted by cruel selfishness and sordid disrespect for religion. His message was stated in the form of a pledge made by God to the people He created:

> Bring ye the whole tithe into my storehouse. And prove
> me now therewith, and see if I won't pour you out a
> blessing that you'll not have room to receive.

Harris took the tithe to mean ten percent of a person's livelihood. He consistently asked his parishioners to turn over a tenth of their salaries or profits to the Lord. They would always receive blessings in excess of whatever money they gave to the church and God.

In fifty years as a minister, he had never seen the Lord go back on that word. He tithed. Many of the members in his congregation followed the teaching. All of his sons and daughters gave their ten percent, some to his own church. It was the most basic of beliefs in Harris' mind.

As Harris read through the beginning of the letter, his faith was reaffirmed. The young man had written that he had accepted the reverend's advice and had begun to tithe what little money was coming into his establishment. In a short while, business began to pick up dramatically. Since he started tithing, he enjoyed enormous box-office success with two features: *Deliverance* and *The Godfather*. The latter film had been expected to gross big, but, as it turned out, both were instant favorites with the college crowd. The people in the university community had rediscovered his cinema. And he believed he could insure their support by reducing his admission price to a dollar for all showings, a marketing tactic he had heard was proving enormously successful at other college area movie houses. Harris' young friend was stunned at the incredible luck that had followed his tithing.

To the young man, it probably seemed like luck. To Harris, it was all part of God's agreement.

Harris was about to read on when he was interrupted by his wife's voice coming from inside the house. It sounded upset.

As he rushed into the house he heard his wife demand, "Vivy, was he hurt badly? What do the doctors say?"

While she was getting her answers, the reverend mouthed the word, "Bob?"

She nodded yes.

Silently, he began to hope it wasn't serious. In fact, he began to pray.

They had received this kind of call so many times before. Harris never understood why his son-in-law, Bob Farrington, continued to drive horses in races after he had suffered so many serious injuries.

The Harrises had always liked Bob Farrington, despite some early reservations. Bob had plucked their daughter out of high school and married her, he had chosen a financially risky career in harness racing, and his religious background had not been all that the Harrises would have liked.

Their first two concerns had evaporated with time. Bob was not only a fine husband and father, but had proven himself a huge success on the nation's racetracks. And the matter of his religious character had been settled as early as 1953.

It was in August of that year when the Harrises' son, Chuckie, had died suddenly from complications arising after some of his baby teeth were pulled. Chuckie was retarded and very much loved by the family, especially Bob. The death of the eight-year-old boy had a deep effect on Farrington spiritually. He surprised the entire family a few weeks later when he expressed the desire to be baptized and declare Christ as his Savior.

The baptism meant a great deal to the Harrises. They cared about Bob more than they could ever show. This concern was on the reverend's mind as his wife shoved the telephone receiver into his hand.

"Now Dad, Bob is going to be all right," Vivian said, repeating what she had reported to her mother. "He had an accident and broke his right shoulder again. The doctor says he'll be fine, though. He'll have to be in the hospital a few weeks . . . in traction. . . ."

"Vivy, Vivy," Harris pleaded, "is it worth all this?"

"Dad," she answered, "this time he says he's going to quit. He's giving up the driving. It was his own decision, and he says he's through. He's going to leave it for the younger men. No more driving. No more accidents."

"Thank God," the reverend replied. "Tell Bob he's doing the right thing. Tell him we pray for him."

"Dad, I will," she promised. "I have to go now . . . the nurse is saying something about changing his room. Listen, Mother can give you the details. Bob'll be fine. That's the important thing. I'll call you again tomorrow. Love you both."

"Goodbye, Vivy," Harris said, hanging up the phone.

"Mother," the reverend said excitedly, "did Vivy tell you the good news? That Bob's going to quit his driving? I've prayed for him to make that decision. Prayed hard and long. It's unfortunate that he's hurt again, of course, but if it means an end to all that danger. . . ."

"I know, Lloyd; you've said it so many times—everything has a way of happening for the best."

"Absolutely," he agreed firmly. "God sees to it."

"He surely does. And now you'd better get cracking or He'll have to see to a new job for you."

Chapter 4

*R*ay Gibson, his two hundred and ten-pound frame planted firmly on the seat of the battered jog cart, was rather hoping his mother wouldn't be watching as he and his two-year-old pacing colt left the barn and headed for the big track down in the cornfield.

But there she was, sure as death and taxes, her head poking out the window on the warm April morning. . . .

"You better slow that colt down, Raymond," Mrs. Lloyd Gibson hollered facetiously. "He won't have any energy left for the workout."

"Aw, Ma, you know damn well that's just his manner," Gibson shouted back. "He's too smart to hurry down to the track when he knows he's got to jog five miles once he gets there."

"Smart like Bret Hanover," Mrs. Gibson jeered.

"Well, he's no Bret, I admit, but I think he's going to make a good racehorse once he sets his mind to it."

"Raymond, if that lazy, shufflin' animal manages to win a race, I'll bake you the biggest custard pie in the history of Monroeville, Indiana."

"I'll hold you to that, Ma."

"Well, I'm not about to begin mixing the crust," Mrs. Gibson offered as a parting shot, laughing heartily.

Gibson dredged up an answering chuckle, but at the same time, slapped the reins against the colt's sides and clucked to him.

The young horse ignored him, continuing his tortoise-like, methodical plod along the weedy path leading to the track.

Raymond L. Gibson was reasonably sure his assessment of the two-year-old was correct, his mother's wrong. Oh, she was right about the colt's surface indolence, Gibson admitted—he was about as sluggish an animal as Gibson had ever encountered. But his mother had not been there when Ray and his dad had broken the horse to harness and jog cart.

Willie had learned his early lessons easier than any other young horse in Ray Gibson's experience. Willie had also grasped the routine of jogging the first time he'd been sent around the crude, half-mile, farm track. And he'd further proven that he possessed a spot of speed in his lanky frame. When and if he chose to flash it.

But, then, Ray Gibson did not mind confessing that he, Ray Gibson, was hardly what you'd term a seasoned harness horseman. He hadn't noticed any Delvin Millers, Stanley Dancers or Billy Haughtons sidling up next to him, seeking his advice.

He was, first and foremost, a farmer, growing corn, beans, wheat, oats and hay on his sixty-seven acre spread about three miles southwest of Monroeville on Rural Route 3. In addition, the thirty-three-year-old Gibson worked the graveyard shift at the Goodrich Rubber Company plant in nearby Fort Wayne. He toiled on the assembly line, helping to turn out tires for the company that had no blimp.

A wife—Mary—and four children—Rodney, Rhonda, Randy and Rae—also placed the usual family demands on his time.

Gibson had entertained no notion of expanding those horizons to include harness racing until his father, Lloyd Gibson, had changed all that by breaking an arm in a racing accident at Greenville, Ohio, in the early 1960s.

Ray had to pitch in and help his disabled father with the breaking and early training of two yearling colts. Out of gratitude, the senior Gibson gave him half-interest in one of the youngsters. Ray Gibson was quickly hooked.

He started driving at the Indiana and Ohio fairs in 1968, suffering through three lean seasons. But in 1971, his thirty-three starts produced fourteen wins, four seconds, seven thirds and $4,036 in purse money.

Like his father, Ray Gibson decided early on that he would breed standardbreds as well as train and drive them. To breed horses you obviously must possess a broodmare—a prospective mother—and Ray found his close to home.

An uncle had bought a pacing-bred mare named Meadow Belle as a riding horse for his young son, but the experiment had not worked out. Meadow Belle had not only been crippled at birth, but also owned a disposition that was downright ornery.

The combination of faults was almost lethal. With the youngster in the saddle, the foul temper would sometimes inspire the mare to rear up, and the faulty rear leg would then cause her to fall over sideways.

Since the uncle did not particularly relish the thought of having a son covered with welts and bruises, he decided to sell the horse.

Ray Gibson bought her for $175.

While Meadow Belle was the daughter of a pedestrian stallion named Meadow Gold, there were traces of royalty— Adios, Maggie Counsel, Abbedale and Volomite—in the back chapters of her pedigree.

Gibson did not have far to go to find a stallion to mate with his new broodmare. His father, located only a few wide pastures away, had a sire called Rambling Rebel in residence at his farm. Sending Meadow Belle to Rambling Rebel was not only handy, but the price was right.

A stud colt arrived in 1968. Ray and Mary Gibson named him Rambling Shorty. A year later, the Meadow Belle-Rambling Rebel mating produced a youngster called Rambling Spook.

Both were promising racehorses, but Ray Gibson had no way of knowing how exceptional they might become when it was time to breed his feisty, lame mare for the third time. By now, Rambling Fury, a young horse his father had trained and driven, was also standing at Lloyd Gibson's budding breeding farm. Ray decided to try the newcomer.

Rambling Fury had been no great shakes as a racehorse, taking a 2:04 2/5—two minutes, four and two-fifths seconds—win record as a three-year-old. But he, too, had a smattering of shiny names in the recesses of his pedigree— Billy Direct, Hal Dale, Scotland, Abbedale and Peter Volo among them.

His prospects as a stallion were every bit as bright as those of his barn-mate, Rambling Rebel, although people in the sport with blue blooded broodmares were not likely to break down the doors to get to either of them.

At 4:30 A.M. on April 18, 1970, Mary Gibson had wandered out to the family's four-stall barn for perhaps the tenth time that night and had witnessed the birth of Meadow Belle's third foal. There were no complications. The colt slipped out of his mother's womb with a minimum of fuss, and was standing on quivering legs, nursing greedily within fifteen minutes. Satisfied, Mrs. Gibson had gone back to bed.

The family called the bay youngster Rambling Willie, registering that name with the United States Trotting Association. The "Rambling" portion of his name was natural, in that all the Gibsons' colts bore that surname. The "Willie" was added only because further identification was needed.

It was clearly an undistinguished name, thoroughly common. But at that time, Willie was a common looking foal, born of common parents, owned by common folks. And he would always be the common man's racehorse, no matter how uncommonly he might race.

Ray Gibson's plan from the beginning was to train and race his horses lightly at the fairs, then sell them if and when the men with shrewd eyes and cash in their pockets turned up to wheel and deal.

With his lifestyle—farming it, working at Goodrich, and raising a young family—he couldn't afford the luxury of holding on to them. Racing at fairs can only be a hobby. But campaigning horses at the professional tracks like Hazel Park in Detroit and Scioto Downs in Columbus requires time, money and expertise. And Ray Gibson possessed none of those prerequisites.

Gibson had already said farewell to Rambling Shorty and was entertaining offers on Rambling Spook. Shorty would go on to take a racing record of 2:01 and earn more than $65,000. Spook, bringing $15,000 to a joyous Ray Gibson when he was sold, would earn in excess of $105,000 for his new owners.

"Don't get attached to this horse," Ray always warned his wife and children, " 'cause he's for sale."

Gibson decided that Rambling Willie would be no exception when he began to train him early in 1972. All his lessons, along with the actual training that followed, were carried out at

Lloyd Gibson's farm, in that the senior Gibson had carved out a pair of training tracks on his property. One was a third-mile oval in an open field. The other was a larger, half-mile track that cut a swathe through tillable acreage that normally bore alternate year crops of corn, beans and hay.

If Ray Gibson made any mistakes along the way, it was the day he decided, almost casually, to have Willie castrated. His father had mentioned that he had asked Dr. John Parker to stop by the farm to geld three of his own colts.

"Hell, long as he's going to be there, why don't you have him cut Willie, too," Ray had directed.

Removing the testicles of stud horses whose bloodlines are not all that blue is not that unusual, especially among smaller breeders who intend to race the horses they produce. Rambling Willie's lineage was hardly spectacular, and Ray Gibson had every intention of racing him. He would be more tractable, more attentive, pleasanter to be around, and less troublesome as a gelding, so the altering was ordered.

Ray Gibson had no regrets.

And both Gibsons, son and father, noticed that Willie seemed to heal faster than the other young victims of the veterinarian's knife.

Willie remained a mystery as he began to leg up for his eventual racing debut. He was bright, intelligent and cheerful, yet made it quite clear to Ray Gibson that he was not fond of training.

His indolence in walking to the track, a trait noticed early and often by Gibson's mother, did not end when he arrived at the dusty oval. He was a reluctant jogger, slogging along with little interest, gazing out at the tilled fields around him. Gibson had to hoot and holler, slap him with the lines, and flick a whip at him to keep him going.

Yet, when he felt like it, Willie would whip along at a dazzling pace, and Ray Gibson, even with his limited background, could recognize the splendor of his gait—the long, rhythmic strides landing on the bumpy track in perfect mesh.

His three-quarter brother, Rambling Spook, had been a smooth-going pacer, but Willie's gait was even silkier, his stride even longer. Then and there, Gibson resolved to "ask a lot of money for him" when the time was ripe.

The "lot of money" would have to be lured through his

performances, not his looks. Willie was a shade taller than the average two-year-old, but his aesthetic advantages ended there. His color was standard bay, his head undistinguished looking, and only a small white ring around his rear, left foot saved him from being totally unmarked. His conformation—the way he stood—was sound and good, though not outstanding.

Going through an auction ring, Rambling Willie would hardly have earned a raised eyebrow. And it was questionable as to how many bids he would have attracted as the auctioneer sang his praises and pleaded for offers.

The frozen ground gave way to mud, which, in turn, became dust as Willie circled the Lloyd Gibson farm track day after day after day. Patches of snow disappeared on the surrounding fields, and each morning marked the return of another vacationing bird as Willie's legs grew stronger, his lung capacity greater. Gradually, almost grudgingly, he produced more speed for his anxious trainer.

By early May of 1972, Ray Gibson was telling his father, "I'd like to race Willie; I think he's about ready."

"You do?" The elder Gibson was surprised.

"Yep."

"What have you been with him?"

"Only two minutes, forty-five seconds. But he's not the kind of horse you can get fast training miles out of. That's why I thought I'd race him. Kind of easy, of course, but he should learn a little in with other horses. Might make a racehorse out of him."

"Those other boys, you know; they'll have been a bit more with their colts," Lloyd Gibson counseled.

"Hell, I know that. But it's only a matinee. I'll be careful so's he don't get hurt none."

"Well, he's your horse, Raymond. . . ."

"I think I'll try him at Celina, Ohio. That's a pretty good little track, and there's a baby race for pacers there on the fourteenth of this month. But do me a favor and don't tell Ma, will you? I want to have that honor, since she never figured I'd get this one to the races."

"You got that wrong," the elder Gibson corrected. "Your mother says you'll never squeeze a win out of that horse." But then he rubbed his chin and added, "On the other hand, maybe you got it right, 'cause, deep down, I don't think she ever believed he'd race a'tall.''

"All I know is—and I'm gonna warn her—that she's gonna owe me a big pie before old Willie gets through.''

The sun was barely up when Ray Gibson coaxed Rambling Willie into a weary looking, two-horse trailer and set out along Route 33 for Celina, a town of some 8,000 citizens near the Ohio-Indiana border.

Gibson, as always, preferred an early start, hoping to get a decent stall for his horse. Late arrivals, of course, drew the dregs at the fairs—housing in barns that were sometimes crumbling with age. The Celina fairground, thankfully, was in better condition than most.

Part of the joy of racing at fairs is renewing acquaintances with other horsemen that travel the same circuit, and Gibson did a lot of that as he was readying Willie for his afternoon race. Hopes were high among many of the harness folks, while others told Raymond tales of potential champions that had gone hellish miles on the training track, only to break down days before they were to make their first start.

Everyone seemed to agree that Dave McClain's youngster, Quick N Steady, was the colt to beat in the afternoon contest.

Gibson was expecting very little from Willie—in fact, had told everyone that—and was not disappointed. Willie faced four rivals in his career debut, a purseless event, and finished fifth and last. The trophy, donated by a local bakery, went to Quick N Steady as expected, with the youngster pacing a mile in 2:23 1/5.

But it was a warm, pleasant afternoon, and Willie managed to stay on the pacing gait all the way, so Gibson was reasonably contented as he headed for home.

Three weeks later, on June 4, Gibson tried him again, this time in a matinee at Portland, Indiana, and Willie looked a mite stronger, finishing fourth in a dash that went in a brisk 2:11 2/5. A week later, racing at Wapakoneta, Ohio, he nearly earned his owner-trainer a custard pie, finishing second in a contest that went 2:13 3/5. Back at Portland on June 18, Willie again finished only a tick or two behind the leader, although only he and two opponents went to post in that one.

"He's getting better with every start," Ray Gibson told his father.

"That he is," the senior Gibson agreed.

"Gonna try him in the big time—Anderson," his son reported.

While it mattered not to Rambling Willie, he made his professional racing debut—competing for a cash prize—on the nation's birthday, July 4, 1972. The whole Gibson clan was out for that one, sampling the midway, touring the exhibits of livestock and produce, sharing a picnic lunch, then settling down in the grandstand to watch Willie.

The young pacer had to go a pair of heats for the first time, meaning he had to race twice on the afternoon card, and he finished fourth to the familiar Quick N Steady in the first dash, then lost narrowly to a youngster called Spoiled Brat in 2:11 in the second.

The Gibsons, weary but happy, rolled down the highway for home with a rapidly improving pacer in the trailer and a check for $163 in Ray Gibson's pocket. Rambling Willie had enjoyed his first payday as a racehorse.

Gibson had never intended to race him either hard or long in his freshman season, and decided to call it quits for the year with a race at Converse, Indiana.

Willie squared off against six other apprentice pacers in another double-dash event and wound up second in both. The times for the two miles were 2:08 and 2:10, and his creditable performances were worth another $186 to the Gibson family.

Willie's first year at the races was over.

Ironically, the date of Rambling Willie's last start as a two-year-old was July 11, 1972. While he was circling the Converse half-mile track, earning the first flicker of interest from the shrewd-eyed horse traders who congregate at the fairs, a famous harness horse driver was lying in the corridor of a Chicago area hospital, waiting for treatment to begin for injuries he'd suffered in a racing wreck that morning.

Chapter 5

*B*ob Farrington stared down at the numbers between his feet. They spun wildly—undecipherably—to the left, then suddenly reversed direction. Back to the left. Again to the right. Slowly losing speed, quickly gaining legibility. When the digits came to a halt, the number on his bathroom scale read 155.

A smile came to his face.

Bob, ole buddy, you're getting fat, he thought. All that good life has put a tire around your waist.

His body was definitely thickening. No longer the strong, lean physique of a long-distance runner. He was twenty pounds heavier than in the years when he dominated his driving rivals on the nation's racetracks.

Yet, he was satisfied, satisfied with everything the extra pounds stood for. They represented a less hectic pace of life. He was finding more time to rediscover his family and close friends. He was enjoying his view from the racetrack stands as son-in-law Jim Curran headed toward his best driving year ever—more than two hundred wins, earning purses in excess of $750,000. There was even time to tune into his beloved ballgames on television.

Farrington no longer spent every waking hour worrying about, working with, and watching over his racing stable. He was driving sparingly. He had plunged into semi-retirement after his last racing accident. And he had made it stick.

It was exactly one year since he had smashed his shoulder into the turf of the Sportsman's Park racetrack. In four days he would celebrate his forty-fourth birthday. He felt rested, contented; he felt great. He couldn't recall being happier. Nor more at peace.

"Viv," he yelled through the bathroom door, "What time is it?"

"Almost 5:00," she responded. 5:00 A.M., she added silently, still full of wonder that she would rise at such an indecent hour for the sole purpose of looking at somebody's horse. Not that she was complaining. Far from it. For years she had seen little of her husband as he dashed frantically about winning races and setting records. Now she saw a great deal more of him, and he was more at ease, happier, always in a good mood. She was glad to accompany him on his horse-buying missions. If only they started a little later in the day.

"We've got to get going," Bob advised.

"I still don't understand it," Vivian protested. "It seems to me that if he wants to sell the horse, he'd wait for us."

"You know how independent us farmers are," Farrington said, grinning. "That Gibson fella, he's racing a horse at Converse today and he wants to get an early start. Only way to get a good stall, he told me. If we're at his farm by 8:00, he'll sell us the Willie horse. Otherwise, he's long gone, headed for the fair. It's as simple as that."

"That's independent, all right," Vivian agreed.

"And don't forget the money," Bob reminded with a snicker. "Has to be in cash. In hundred dollar bills. I'm Bob Farrington, six-time national driving champ, but he won't accept my check. Cash only, he says. And we had to scurry a bit to round it up, didn't we, Hon?"

"Scurry? *Scrounge* is more like it. Tapping the savings account, borrowing from friends, raiding the safe deposit box. . . ."

"A real pain," Farrington said, nodding. "This Rambling Willie horse had better be everything that Squeaky says he is."

"Squeaky" was Paul Sherwood, a veteran caretaker with the Ohio-based stable of Gene Riegle. Squeaky, whose high-pitched voice—it turned into a shrill whistle when his emotions were aroused—had earned him his nickname, was an old friend of the Farrington family and a canny, crafty judge of horseflesh.

The rangy groom, who could have been a trainer in his own right had he the inclination, had spotted a promising looking three-year-old pacer named Rambling Willie racing on the Indiana fair circuit. The horse was sound, possessed raw speed, and was in inexperienced hands—precisely the kind, Squeaky knew, that his friend Bob Farrington cherished.

As for Farrington, he had benefited from Sherwood's counsel in the past, and generally acted with dispatch when the caretaker called with a recommendation. It was Squeaky's most recent call, in fact, that was sending Bob and Vivian on their predawn pilgrimage to northeastern Indiana, where Rambling Willie was on display at a small farm outside of Monroeville. On display, that is, if the Farringtons arrived by 8:00 A.M.

The Farrington auto was winding through Merrillville, Indiana, when Bob glanced over at his wife. Vivian was dozing, lulled to sleep by the steady hum of tires on the highway, her pretty head cradled in the corner formed by the car door and the back of her seat. The craggy-faced horseman felt a wave of affection wash over him as his eyes returned to the gunmetal gray highway in front of him.

Vivian was as game as they come, he knew. Always had been, always would be. She'd held down a pair of jobs—secretary for a radio station and bookkeeper for the local waterworks—during the lean years, when he was trying to crack the harness game. She'd never complained when home was a single room in some boarding house, or maybe a ramshackled tackroom. And she'd never groused, never argued, when he'd stripped the last $500 from their savings to bring home some creaking, bad-legged horse that he thought might do them a bit of good.

She'd put up with a lot over the years, he knew, and overlooked birthdays were included. In the early days, he hadn't possessed the cash to buy her the gift she deserved. In later years, when success had settled on him, he was generally too busy to remember. It hurt him to recall the time she'd set the combination on his new travel case at 7-23, the date of her birthday. And, if his memory was accurate, he'd managed to miss that year, too.

This year—1973—was different, however. Rested, less busy, with more time on his hands, he'd remembered. It was only a dozen days into the future, her birthday, and he was determined to make up for all the years of neglect. He wanted something special for her, something spectacular and unusual, and as the headlights of his Oldsmobile slashed through the gathering light, an idea was forming.

The Olds was approaching the community of Wanatah as the breaking dawn unveiled the flat Indiana farmland bordering the highway. The territory was familiar to Bob. Wanatah preceded Hanna. The next town would be Hamlet. Then Grovertown. Then Donaldson. The road continued on into the state of Ohio, where Farrington normally took a right at Williamstown and headed south for the tiny town of Richwood.

Richwood was the typical Central Ohio farm community—cozy, clean and countrified. If it was different in any way, that difference had to do with the Farrington family—father Louis, wife Frances, and sons Rolland, Richard, Bradley and Robert, along with their wives. The Farringtons, en masse, owned and operated a four hundred-acre farm some seven miles west of Richwood. Like their neighbors, they shared pleasures. And one of the Farrington clan's greatest pleasures was also its business—the racing of harness horses.

The family's connection with horses had taken root in Rugby, England. The earliest patriarchs were blacksmiths in the English town. Above the door of the clan's shop was hung a sign advertising: *"Farriery Done Here.'* And from the sign had come the family's name: Farrington.

The most recent generation of the family—Louie and the boys—had never decided to hang a sign above the gate to their farm. But if they had, it probably would have read: *"Everything Done Here."* For the family-run equine operation was practically self-sufficient, depending upon outsiders for only the equipment necessary for racing—jog carts, sulkies, harnesses, bits, hopples and the like.

The Farrington racing stable was the biggest of its day, one of the largest ever. Bob Farrington and his father ran the vast family enterprise from their respective command posts in Chicago and Richwood. They were united daily by the telephone, and twice a week by motorized van. The vehicle shuttled a constant supply of horses, hay, straw, oats and equipment back and forth between the two operations. The usual route was the familiar Highway 30.

At the Chicago end of the shuttle was the racing stable. It usually contained fifty standardbred racehorses trained to their sharpest competitive edge. Another group of fifty resided on the Richwood farm as a squad of substitutes ready for shipment to the metropolitan racing arena to replace their race-weary stablemates. A third wave of fifty horses was also on and around the farm, some of them in various stages of recovery from lameness or illness; others, broodmares waiting to foal.

The fifty-horse racing division at the track was broken down into three sub-strings. They all campaigned under the Farrington banner, but each operated as an independent entity. Richard Farrington commanded one. The others were the responsibility of assistant trainers such as John Miritello, Harold Brown or Al Bernard. At his peak, Bob Farrington drove *all* the stable's trotters and pacers.

For Bob, the day began at 6:30 A.M. and never seemed to end. He had overall charge of all fifty horses at the track, individually training the stable's "outlaws" and problem animals. When he was not on the track, he accompanied a veterinarian on daily tours of the barn. It was generally late afternoon by the time he arrived home, giving him time for a brief nap, telephone reports to owners of horses in his stable, and a quick dinner. Then it was back to the track for an evening full of driving.

It was not unusual to see his red and gray silks behind a trotter or pacer seven, eight or even nine times a night. He quickly began to win two or three contests an evening. Occasionally, he would score four wins. Once in a great while he posted five—even six—victories. Such feats were rare in harness racing before the start of the Farrington era.

Two hundred and fifty miles southeast of the Chicago station—at the other end of the shuttle—was the Richwood farm, where activities were easily as frenetic. The portly, cigar-chomping Louis Farrington was the trail boss there, managing the family's four hundred acres, plus another two thousand leased acres where Rolland Farrington raised the oats, hay, corn and straw used by the Farrington horses.

Ninety-nine stalls, four turnout paddocks, and a half-mile training track were all part of the family's farm. The hundred horses in residence were segregated by need. Some relaxed in their stalls or the paddocks, recovering from injuries. Others were busy on the training track, being sharpened before shipment to the races. Mares heavy with foals roamed through the fields. Every horse was expected to contribute to the stable's ultimate goal—making money.

In addition to their everyday tasks, every member of the

family—Louie, Bob, Richard, Rolland and Bradley, who raced a private stable in Ohio, but handled some of the Farrington horses as well—was expected to keep an eagle eye out for young horses that might benefit from the Farrington touch. The family was especially interested in buying inexperienced horses being handled by inexperienced horsemen. And that was the reason Bob Farrington was steering his powerful auto along Rural Route 2, a couple of miles outside of Monroeville, Indiana, at 7:50 A.M. on July 11, 1973.

"Honey," said his wife, yawning and stretching, "I just dreamed about a horse with one white leg. Do you suppose it's got anything to do with Rambling Willie?"

"I don't know," her husband offered.

Bob was often skeptical of her references to—and reliance upon—dreams. Vivian was a student of extrasensory perception and the supernatural, and her faith in prayer was absolute. Her husband was more at home with things he could see, taste and smell, although Vivian had amazed him at times.

"I think it does," she stated flatly.

"Well, at the very least, you only dreamed of one white leg," he responded. "You know the old horsemen's adage, 'One white leg inspect him, two white legs reject him, three white legs sell him to your foes, four white legs feed him to the crows.' "

"Just one white leg, and we're going to like Willie," Vivian predicted.

Farrington did not have time to answer. He was steering the car through the front gate of the Gibsons' property, stopping alongside a ranch-style brick house of obvious recent vintage.

A chunky, young man of about five feet, eleven inches rounded the corner and advanced toward the auto. "Got to be the son, Ray. The guy that owns the horse," Bob alerted Vivian.

They were quickly out of the vehicle, shaking hands with Raymond Gibson and meeting his wife, Mary, and parents, Lloyd and Dorothy Gibson. "I suppose you'd like to see Willie," Ray Gibson volunteered, leading a single file parade into a medium-sized barn at the rear of the property.

Farrington's practiced eyes, squinting a little as they adjusted from the sunlight outside, surveyed the horse's stall before they focused on the animal. He noticed immediately that the horse was standing ankle deep in soiled straw, and was not surprised. Farmers rarely had either the time or the inclination to give their horses the care that professional horsemen do. Sometimes it was astounding the way a horse would respond to the better treatment offered by the professionals.

Bob's gaze then shifted to the animal. A bit bigger than average, he thought. Conformation seemed reasonably good. Broad, barreled chest. Appeared to have a pleasant disposition.

"Can we take him outside?" the trainer asked.

"Sure thing," the younger Gibson said agreeably.

Out in the early morning sunshine, Farrington's inspection began in earnest. The four Gibsons looked on with a kind of mixed admiration and apprehension as the old pro went to work. Farrington grabbed the horse's tail and looked over his rump as though he were viewing him from the seat of a sulky. Dropping the tail, he ran a hand down the gelding's hip. Then he repeated the action on the horse's other side.

He faced the horse head on, studying his head, then putting a half-opened hand in the crook between the head and the neck. For a full two minutes, he fastened his eyes on the horse's front legs, observing them from some six feet away. His face was totally void of expression, like a poker player's, as he went to work on the legs.

He checked the rear pair first, running a hand down the length of each, looking for signs of a curb, the painful bulging of ligaments or tendons behind the leg. The only thing he found was a narrow band of white hair just above the left hoof—Vivian's white foot. He could feel his wife's eyes on him, knew that she had spotted the strip of white, and was confident that Rambling Willie had already passed her test. But he gave no indication that the pacer had survived *his* examination.

He headed back to the front of the horse, checking the legs, poking, prodding and squeezing each knee, and searching for a touch of heat or softness in the tendons. He discovered none. Then he lifted each foot, examining the horse's hooves, and noticed that he was shod with keg shoes, far more appropriate for a work animal than a racehorse.

"Can I see him move?" he asked the younger Gibson.

"Sure," said Gibson as he tugged at Willie's lead shank,

forcing him to jog. While it wasn't much of a test, Farrington could readily see that his gait was reasonably good, that the spread of his legs was proper.

"Looks good," he commented to Ray Gibson, who was puffing a little after leading the horse up and down the driveway a couple of times.

"Then you want him?" Gibson probed.

"Fifteen thousand?" Farrington asked.

"Fifteen thousand."

"Seems a little high," the trainer commented, meaning it. At the time, Farrington felt $10,000 was about right for the pacer.

"Like I told you on the phone, the price is firm. Fifteen thousand," Gibson said. "Cash," he added.

"Cash," Bob repeated, smiling.

"You want him at that price?"

"I'll take him," Farrington said softly.

The four Gibsons, en masse, exhaled. Vivian Farrington merely smiled; she had known for some time that her husband was buying the horse.

"I'll get the money," Bob said, heading for the trunk of his car and returning with a briefcase. "Looks like ransom money," he offered lightly as he opened the case, set it on the auto's hood, then gently pushed it toward Raymond Gibson.

Gibson handed Rambling Willie's lead shank to his father, then began to count the cash—one hundred and fifty one-hundred dollar bills. Nervously, he lost the count twice, finally turning the task over to his wife. By this time, there were stacks of bills in Mary Gibson's hand, on the hood of the car, and in the briefcase. Suddenly a gust of wind scattered the bills all over the yard like a small pile of dry leaves. The Gibsons and the Farringtons hustled to retrieve them. Somehow the counting was completed. Rambling Willie belonged to the Farringtons.

"And you'll ship him to my barn in Chicago," Bob reminded Ray Gibson.

"I'll do it," Gibson promised.

A handshake all around, and the Farringtons were back in their car, the vehicle pointing back to Chicago.

"He's beautiful," Vivian said with animation.

"Looks like a racehorse," Bob offered matter-of-factly.

"And did you notice the white foot?" she pressed.

"That's the only reason I bought him," her husband said facetiously.

"That'll be the day," Vivian scoffed.

"You really like him, huh?"

"Like him? Bob, I *love* him."

"Then I'll tell you what, Mrs. Farrington," Bob said grandly, lovingly. "Since your birthday's only twelve days away, and since I've remembered it for a change, and since you've never, ever had a racehorse of your own, I'll give you half of Rambling Willie. As a birthday present. You can be partners on him with Lloyd Arnold. How's that sound to you?"

"Are you serious?"

"Of course I'm serious. Your name goes on him. Yours and Lloyd's, more than likely. Half of what he earns will go to you. But, then, half the expenses on him will be yours, too. Maybe then you'll get an idea of what my owners go through."

There was silence in the car. Farrington looked at his wife to determine whether she was shedding happy tears or having second thoughts. At length, she fastened shining eyes on him and said, "Bob, I've got such a good feeling about Willie. I think he's going to be a champion."

"No, Honey," her husband amended. "Remember, we came to buy a cheap horse. He's going to be just another racehorse, probably a claimer."

"No, no, Bob. He's going to be a great one. I just know it. He's going to be a champion!"

"Well, Lord knows I could use a champion," Farrington said placatingly.

"He does, you know. He really does."

"Who does? Who does what?" Bob asked, mystified.

"The *Lord*," Vivian replied. "The Lord knows if Willie's going to be a great horse. And I know He'll make him a champion, if we ask Him."

"Oh, Viv, you and that faith. . . ." Bob started to chide. Then he thought better of it and simply grinned. "You could be right."

"I am, Bob. I am. You'll see."

Chapter 6

*I*f ever a man were ripe to buy a racehorse, it was Paul Seibert of Cincinnati.

Seibert, tallish, with a shock of nearly white hair, spent his days as an advertising display specialist with the Spare Change Stores, Inc., a string of women's apparel shops in Ohio. By night, like a Clark Kent shedding his mild manner for a crime-busting splurge as Superman, Seibert became the consummate harness racing fan. A man who could—and did—attend the races almost every evening without ever growing weary of it.

His friends claimed that he had never married because of an inherent fear that a spouse—no matter how yielding, how tolerant—might, even by accident, put the tiniest of crimps in his style. And Seibert's style was to rush home from work, swallow a quick supper, yank off his tie, don a nondescript looking raincoat, and point his car toward the racetrack.

As a super fan, he liked everything about a track, *any track*—the thrills of the betting windows, the camaraderie of fellow fans, the general din, the subtle, mixed aroma of stale popcorn and manure pervading the night air, the mysteries of the racing program, the fascination of the backstretch and its residents, the excitement of opening and closing nights, and of all the nights between.

Lebanon and Latonia Raceways near Cincinnati were his main playgrounds, but on any given weekend Seibert could be spotted in the grandstands of tracks spreading from New York City to Los Angeles. He was particularly fond of the Chicago area tracks, and he could—and sometimes did—drive the highways connecting the Queen and Windy Cities in his sleep.

The ultimate harness racing fan is never content until his or her name is on the registration papers of a trotter or pacer, and Paul Seibert was no exception.

In 1957 he paid $800 for a pacing mare the seller had recently given $100 for. The mare promptly died. Later in the year, he nursed an ailing pacer back to health, lost him in a claiming race, and the horse immediately reeled off four straight wins for the new owner. In 1958, sight unseen, he purchased a five-year-old trotter named Scotonia at a dispersal sale and learned later that a veterinarian had predicted the horse would never race again.

But veterinarians have been known to be wrong, and this one was. Scotonia did race, although not up to Seibert's inflated expectations. One night, dejected after his trotter had missed the winner's circle again, he walked back to the barn and found a young man sitting on a tack trunk nearby.

"Your horse raced real good tonight," the man commented.

Seibert recognized him as Bob Farrington, a training and driving regular at Lebanon Raceway the past couple of seasons, but a horseman who was about to graduate from the small Ohio track to bigger and better things.

"Yeah, but he never seems to win," Seibert replied.

"Finished a strong second," the young horseman pointed out. "I'll take a barn full of horses like that."

Seibert was flattered. "Would you like to have him?" he asked.

"In my stable? Sure."

"Then you got him. You're his trainer."

Before the horse could be transferred to the Farrington barn, however, Seibert had second thoughts. He felt sorry for his old trainer, Gerry Sterritt, and went to Farrington to try and cancel the agreement. After some hemming and hawing, he explained the situation. Farrington shrugged his shoulders, grinned, and said, "Hey, don't worry about it."

As expected, Bob Farrington, the young star on the rise, later left Lebanon, shipping his growing stable to Brandywine Raceway, Wilmington, Delaware.

With Lebanon closing for the season, Seibert hunted another racing home for Scotonia and decided to send him on to Brandywine with trainer Charlie Cookson. "But I want Bob

Farrington to drive him," he stipulated.

Scotonia had been trotting the Ohio track in the neighborhood of 2:08. The first time Farrington drove him, the trotter scored a 2:05 4/5 victory over Brandywine's old and sluggish half-mile track.

Seibert transferred the horse to Farrington's burgeoning barn, and a close and lasting relationship began between the owner and the trainer.

From 1959 through 1971, Paul Seibert and Bob Farrington collaborated on more than two dozen horses, with Seibert generally owning them and Farrington doing the training and driving. Occasionally, they went partners on one, sharing the expense, sharing the profits.

Seibert was never one of Farrington's major patrons. He simply didn't have the money to fill that role, much as he yearned to. But there were always two or three Seibert horses down the long row of Farrington stalls, giving the owner an excellent excuse to zip up to Chicago, where Farrington eventually settled with his herd.

Paul was both his patron and his friend throughout Bob's meteoric ascendancy to the very peak of the standardbred sport. A kidder, a kibitzer, a man with a thundering, infectious laugh, Seibert served as a kind of comic relief as Farrington scraped and clawed to reach and remain at the top. And Paul's reward was the fact that Bob never changed, never got the big head, never abandoned or diminished the friendship, as he ruled the racing front in the mid-1960s.

Paul was aboard the Farrington rocket when one of harness racing's most remarkable mergers took place in 1964—the union of businessman Lloyd Arnold with the Farrington family stable.

Arnold, a towering, slender man with a slashing, captivating grin and a breezy personality, had come out of Douds, Iowa, like a genial tornado to amass varying fortunes from cattle dealing, Iowa real estate, and commodities.

Based in Chicago, and long infatuated with harness racing, he had horses with top flight horsemen such as Harry Burright and Stanley Banks, but watched with interest as Bob Farrington exploded up through the ranks to eclipse not only Burright and Banks, but all the horsemen plying their trade in and around the Windy City.

Arnold's racing roots traced all the way back to the Iowa fair circuits, but he had never subscribed to the popular and rather accurate premise that it was next to impossible to make money racing horses. In Arnold's mind, that was nonsense, an old wives' tale. He was intrigued with Bob Farrington because Farrington not only shared his positive approach, but was proving it every day and night with his horses.

If a horse failed to show a profit in the Farrington barn, you barely had time to say farewell to the animal. Making money was the name of the Farrington game.

It was also the name of the Arnold game.

The Farrington-Arnold merger was almost inevitable. It commenced when Arnold sought out the Red Man and proposed that they buy a horse in partnership. The horse, a mare called Miss Ohio Time, showed a profit at the end of the season. Then all of Arnold's horses went to Farrington, and the Farrington Stable-Arnold Cattle Company became a mouthful of household words in harness racing circles.

For nearly a decade, the diminutive driver and the gangly businessman bought, swapped, claimed and sold trotters and pacers in such profusion that stablehands could barely keep track of them. Stable bookkeepers had an even rougher time of it.

The two were not content to restrict their wheeling and dealing to American shores, but invaded foreign lands as well. Dick Farrington was dispatched to France and came home with a trio of trotters. Bob and Lloyd toured Australia and New Zealand, buying horses as they went. At the conclusion of the tour, a chartered plane carrying forty-nine new Farrington-Arnold standardbreds soared high over the Pacific Ocean, with Chicago as its destination.

The hard-driving, free-wheeling Farrington-Arnold combination produced no colt champions. For an excellent reason. The duo purchased no colts to speak of, since the odds against making money with young horses were—and are—lamentably high. And colt racing meant travel, which was out of the question. Farrington, with his barns bursting at the seams with horses, needed a permanent base in order to get them raced.

While great young standardbred champions like Bret Hanover, Nevele Pride and Most Happy Fella ended up in other hands, bringing fame and fortune to their owners and trainers, Farrington and Arnold were doing just fine with such fleet and wealthy raceway stars as Hasti Jim, Dancing David, Easy Prom, Harry's Frosty Aire, Robb Ranger, Sterling's Hank, Meteore II, Yellow Knife, The Grumbler and Shad Hanover.

Eventually, the operation grew so large that strings of trotters and pacers did have to be sent on the road. To New York City. To Brandywine Raceway. To California. And when the first string—the elite of the stable—was involved, Bob Farrington often went with them. Invariably, he returned to Chicago with another track driving championship trophy to add to his collection.

It was a three-ring circus, with some dazzling action transpiring in every ring. The harness racing world had never seen the likes of it before, and may never again should the sport continue another thousand years.

Through it all, Bob Farrington remained Bob Farrington—taciturn, unassuming, unaffected, forever the country boy who only seemed to be visiting the big time as a sort of vacation from the farm.

Lloyd Arnold held his own, too, breezing through the sport with the big grin splitting his face, dispensing geniality and charm like a John D. Rockefeller spreading dimes. He was popular around the Farrington barn, and his friendship with Bob quickly spilled over to assistant trainers and caretakers working for the stable, as well as to other owners with horses camped in the Farrington headquarters.

In Paul Seibert's case, Arnold not only offered friendship, but tips on the commodities market as well. And one bit of advice to Seibert would come back to haunt Lloyd Arnold for years into the future.

Paul Seibert, the inveterate horse player, had enjoyed a big night at the track in the Autumn of 1971, going home with something bordering on a thousand dollars profit in his poke. When he told Lloyd Arnold about his score, Arnold pointed out that "found money" should be reinvested.

"Let me put it into pork bellies for you and maybe we can run it up to something," the lanky businessman advised.

Seibert's racetrack windfall was sent on to the Chicago Market Exchange.

Within a year and a half, Arnold had parlayed Seibert's thousand into $7,900, and Seibert wanted out. "I want to buy a horse," he explained. "I haven't owned one in more than a year and I'm getting awful itchy."

"I can understand *that*," Arnold laughed. "I'll see that you get a check."

The money was burning a hole in Paul Seibert's pocket in the Spring of 1973. He was yearning to buy a standardbred, and he badgered Bob Farrington about it.

"I'm looking. I'm looking," Farrington told him, but that seemed to be the end of it. Farrington, naturally, had to give preference to Lloyd Arnold, his big owner, and Paul understood that. But surely there must be a trotter or a pacer out there for old Paul. . . .

Then Claude Harvey called Seibert. "A little bird told me you're looking to buy a horse," Harvey fished.

"The bird told you right. What've you got?"

Harvey, an old friend, was a cattle dealer and part time harness horseman. He got around a lot and made it his business to know where one might pick up a promising horse at a decent price.

"There's a green, three-year-old pacer racing on the Indiana fair circuit that might be bought right," he told Seibert. "He's a three-quarter brother to my Rambling Shorty; in fact, same guy's got him. The fella's an amateur, don't know too much about shoeing or rigging a horse, and a smart guy might be able to step the colt up considerable."

"Sounds awful good," Seibert said quickly. "What do you figure we've got to give for him?"

"I think he can be had for $10,000. I believe I could have bought him last year for $3,500, but the guy that's got him—fella named Gibson up in Monroeville, Indiana—has had some success with him and figures he's got a good one on his hands."

"We'd go partners on him, you and me?"

"Right. Five thousand each."

"Count me in," Seibert said, but added, "I'd like to give him to Jim Curran, Bob Farrington's son-in-law. You have any objections to that?"

"None," Harvey replied agreeably. "I'll be seeing that Gibson fella over at the Anderson, Indiana, Fair next week, and maybe I can close the deal then."

"Great," Seibert offered enthusiastically. "By the way,

Claude," he added, "what's the colt's name?"

"Hell, I don't know if I can remember that. It's Rambling something or other—them Gibsons, they name all them things Rambling this or that. This one's Willie, I think. Yeah, that's it—Rambling Willie."

It was a long week for Paul Seibert, waiting for Harvey to call. And when the cattle dealer did phone, it was with bad news.

"That son-of-a-gun Gibson won a heat with him in 2:07 2/5 at Anderson, and now he's jacked the price up to $15,000," he reported.

"You think it's too much?" Seibert probed.

"I do," said Harvey. "The colt's got no breeding, to speak of. He's not eligible to anything. . . ."

"You know best," Seibert admitted.

"Let's forget him," Harvey recommended.

"Well, I'm still in the market. . . ."

"I know it, Paul. I know it. Something'll come along."

It would be three weeks before someone would call Paul Seibert about a horse again.

The caller would be Bob Farrington.

The horse would be Rambling Willie.

When Farrington bought Willie from Raymond Gibson on July 11, 1973, he fully intended for fifty percent of the horse to go to Lloyd Arnold. That's the way their partnership worked; one would find a horse to his liking, then call the other to get his approval, each party owning half of the newcomer. In this instance, Bob had given half of Willie to Vivian. But he saw no reason why Arnold would not join Vivian in a partnership. He figured, in fact, that Arnold would get a kick out of it. So he phoned Lloyd. And he phoned Lloyd. And he phoned Lloyd.

A journalist, describing Lloyd Arnold in one of racing's leading periodicals, wrote of him, "If you need to locate him, you must be prepared to contact a cornfield in Iowa, a track in California, a training center in Florida, a horse auction in Harrisburg, a state fairground in Illinois, or any one of a hundred other sites where his travels take him."

While the writer may have had trouble locating and contacting the elusive Mr. Arnold, Bob Farrington rarely had that problem. Because they owned scores of horses together, and were constantly adding to or subtracting from the total, they were in almost daily contact. They were, that is, except for a brief period when Rambling Willie paced into the Farringtons' lives.

A pair of weeks went by. Farrington tried to phone his partner from time to time, all the while believing that Arnold would either appear in Chicago or phone. But he did not.

"You know," Farrington told his wife, "we've got to get an owner for the other half of that Willie horse. He's ready to race and we've got to get his papers straightened out."

"Do you suppose that Lloyd would mind it if someone else were to be my partner, if someone else were to own the other half?" Vivian asked.

"Lloyd mind? I doubt it. The colt looks to be just another claiming horse."

"Then why don't you call Paul?" she suggested. "The price for half of Willie is $7,500, and that's exactly what he wants to spend."

"Makes sense," Farrington said.

Paul Seibert wasn't home, either. But to Paul's everlasting good fortune, his mother was. "I'll have him call you, Bob," she promised.

Sensing that it involved a horse, an anxious Paul Seibert returned the call moments after he arrived home from work. "You find me something?" he demanded.

"Well, I bought this three-year-old pacer over in Indiana and I need a partner for Vivian on him. But I got to tell you the truth, Paul, I think I gave $5,000 too much for him. Had to go to $15,000. . . ."

Seibert had an eerie feeling. "What's his name?" he interrupted.

"Name? Why, they call him Rambling Willie."

"I'll take him," Paul replied instantly.

Chicago area harness drivers honor Bob Farrington, who, in 1964, became the first driver in history to score 300 wins in a year.

Below, the Reverend C. L. Harris, pastor of the West Mansfield, Ohio, Church of Christ—Rambling Willie's church.

A family portrait — Bob, Karen and Vivian Farrington — during the Red Man's first batch of glory years, the 1960s. *William B. Owens Association photo.*

Below, the market where the Reverend C. L. Harris worked part-time for many years.

A young Rambling Willie.

Everybody had to pitch in during the early stages of Bob's career, including daughter Karen and wife Vivian.

Below, the first "home" owned by the Farringtons. Things would get better.

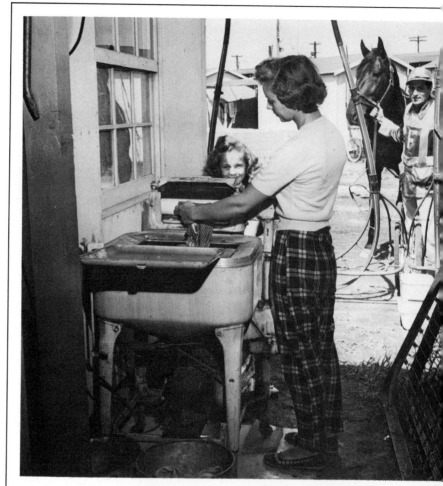

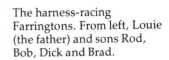
The harness-racing Farringtons. From left, Louie (the father) and sons Rod, Bob, Dick and Brad.

Below, while Rambling Willie was hardly a handsome horse, Al Bernard liked him because "he looked and moved like a racehorse."

The Farrington homestead
farm at Richwood, Ohio.

Below, co-owner Paul
Seibert visits his favorite
pacer.

The Reverend Harris' home.

Below, Willie (7) was a crowd favorite from his earliest starts, his powerful stretch drives endearing him to fans.

Willie dealt similarly with all track conditions — fast, good, muddy or sloppy — as he won almost 45 per cent of his career starts through 1980.

Below, Rambling Willie, a winner all of his life, rarely needed great urging to maintain a lead to the wire.

Chapter 7

*R*ambling Willie, the new addition to the Bob Farrington stable, arrived at Maywood Park with all the pomp and circumstance of an Army recruit showing up for the start of basic training at Fort Dix, New Jersey, during World War II.

Chances are, no one would have remembered his arrival at all had he been delivered at the proper time. As it was, the vehicle bearing him had turned up after the stable gate had closed for the day, requiring a call to Al Bernard, Farrington's top assistant. Bernard, mumbling and grumbling most of the way, had to supervise his unloading outside the gate, then walk him all the way to the Farrington barn.

"I doubt like hell you're gonna be worth all this trouble," Bernard commented sourly to the horse as he pulled him along by a lead shank. "Just another mane and tail," he ventured, choosing racetrack vernacular to describe an ordinary looking horse from which only ordinary things were expected.

Bernard's practiced eye had checked Willie out even as the horse was being backed down the ramp from the trailer. He'd seen a tallish colt with chocolate-like color, a head that seemed a mite too long, and a chest that was reasonably broad and muscled. He'd also noticed a white ring around the coronet of the colt's left, rear leg and had made a mental note of it. With fifty horses in the stable, compounded by a constant turnover, he and the rest of the Farrington assistants needed all the help they could muster in keeping them straight.

"Just another mane and tail," he repeated churlishly as he and Willie approached the red and gray-trimmed Farrington barn.

A pair of caretakers popped out of stalls to greet the pair. "Who you got there?" one inquired.

"Nosy bugger, ain't ya," Bernard replied testily.

"Just interested, Al. That's all."

"Name's Rambling Willie," the trainer said, removing the edge from his voice.

"Bob claim him?"

"Naw. Bob found this champion in a cornfield over in Indiana. Now quit playing *Twenty Questions* and give me a hand. Take him down and put him in that empty stall next to the big trotting mare. I got to figure out a groom to put on him."

Bernard headed for the tackroom that served as the stable office. Once through the screen door, he drew a cup of coffee from a large urn, snorted as he noticed the age and color of the brew, then lowered himself into a rickety chair that saw duty as the partner of a much-marred, paper-strewn desk. Then he let his mind wander down through the roster of caretakers currently working for the stable, remembering that the caretaking staff changed about as often as the Farrington horses. By the time he took his final pull on the cup, setting it down on the desk with a solid thud, he had settled on Sandy Smith as the groom for Rambling Willie.

Sandy Smith, a rather fleshy girl with a pretty face, was about twenty years old and had impressed Bernard during her months on the stable's payroll. She was both ambitious and dedicated. She was also one of the few Farrington stablehands with only one horse in her care, the second having been claimed from the stable a week earlier.

Her only drawback, the trainer remembered, was the fact that she seemed undecided about her future. One day she talked of her love of horses and of her desire to spend her life with them; the next she was telling anybody who would listen of her plan to return to college, to finish art school.

But it would be Sandy, Bernard decided, setting out to find her.

Rambling Willie, the stable crew learned quickly, was not an easy horse to jog and train. Bob Farrington was the first to take him onto the track—it was his policy to be the first to handle a new horse in the stable—and he found him to be both lazy and moody. But it took the veteran horseman only a moment to spot Willie's flawless gait, and he was smiling when he returned to the barn. "Might have a decent one here," he volunteered to Willie's new caretaker.

Sandy Smith wasn't so sure in her early days with Willie. She enjoyed working with him in the stall; he was pleasant, playful, intelligent and obliging. But he gave her fits on the jogging track. He would roll along on the pacing gait for a while, then break into a run. Occasionally, he would transfer smoothly from the pace to the trot, then slow to a walk. He was afraid of everything he saw on the track—watering trucks, tractors tugging harrows or drags, other horses, birds and shadows—shying from them, breaking stride.

Sandy had trouble controlling him, and sometimes, frustrated, she would steer him back to the barn before his jog miles were completed, with the sterner Al Bernard then taking over to complete the training session.

Despite his erratic behavior on the track, Sandy quickly grew to worship Willie. And she quickly commenced to spoil him, feeding him lemon drops, peppermints, apples, peaches, and a wide assortment of other treats.

Vivian Farrington was no more stringent, no more benevolent, showing up at Willie's stall with her own stock of desserts. Willie was Vivian's first horse, and she intended to make the most of it. Spoil him rotten, if she chose.

Paul Seibert arrived to view his new pacer, looked him over from every angle, and pronounced him, "Beautiful. A great looking horse." Al Bernard, holding Willie by the halter while Paul admired him, snickered softly. Al did not consider Willie a handsome horse, although he had begun to appreciate him more as the days went by. Al liked him because he "looked and moved like a racehorse."

Another trainer on the grounds was also smitten with the new Farrington pacer. The problem was, Walter Paisley was thoroughly convinced that Rambling Willie was still residing at the Gibson farm back in Indiana. And still infinitely available for purchase.

One morning, when heavy rain brought training to a halt, Paisley strolled over to Farrington's horse headquarters and

began to crow about the magnificent pacer he had uncov-
ered—and was about to buy—out in the hustings.

"Now, I admit, you've beat me a dozen times in the past,
Red Man," he told Farrington. "You're the master at turning up
the good ones, and you're the guy with the fat check book. But
I tell ya, I got you this time. This promising sucker is headed for
old Walter's barn."

"What's his name?" Farrington inquired casually.

"No way I'm telling you that, Red Man."

"Where's he at?"

"Tell you the state, but nothing more. Indiana."

"Wouldn't be Rambling Willie, would it?"

Paisley's jaw sagged. Farrington started to chuckle, then
laugh, then roar. "Come over here," he said, holding his sides
with laughter. "I want you to meet somebody."

The stable boss was spending more time on Willie than he
had intended. Farrington was retraining the colt, teaching him
to shed his fear of the objects his young eyes observed on the
track. It was understandable the colt would be wary of trucks
and tractors, things he had never seen on the Gibsons' farm
track, but it was imperative that the phobia end. And when it
did, Farrington declared him ready to race.

A conditioned race tailored for young, inexperienced pacers like himself was selected for Willie. The purse for the
contest was $2,500, with the usual harness racing split to apply:
fifty percent to the winner, twenty-five percent for second,
twelve for third, eight for fourth, and five for fifth.

Vivian Farrington dressed with extra care that night. Vivian was always a fashion plate, and her husband encouraged it.
Bob was convinced he was married to the best-looking,
best-groomed lady at the racetrack, and few of the backstretch people or folks who frequented the clubhouse argued
the point.

Bob, on the other hand, was a horseman of a different
color. Or of several different, clashing colors, if Vivian did not
take the time to lay out his clothes for him. He had little interest
in styles or fashions, other than those that covered the slender,
graceful frame of his wife.

Vivian and Paul Seibert decided to view Willie's race from
the Maywood Park clubhouse restaurant. Vivian loved the

races, loved to dress up and have dinner at the track. In Paul Seibert, she had a soul mate, though Paul much preferred a dollar seat in the grandstand to a lavishly spread table in the clubhouse.

But, then, Paul was a special case, Vivian knew. Somewhere Paul had heard—and accurately, too—that several American harness tracks had obliged a few addicted race-goers who had stipulated in their wills that their remains be cremated and sprinkled around the racing ovals they loved so much. Paul liked to joke that it seemed like a logical end for him.

While Vivian and Seibert were nervously toying with steaks in the clubhouse, Bob Farrington was in the paddock, the tightly guarded area where horses are protectively restricted until the race. It was a big night, a busy night for him. Jim Curran, the stable's regular driver, was recovering from a severe ankle injury. Farrington was down to drive a trotter in the first race, then handle Rambling Willie in his nighttime debut in the third. Imagine, he thought, two races on the same night! He could recall evenings when he'd driven the entire Maywood program.

Sandy Smith was back at the barn dressing Willie— putting on his racing equipment—and a problem had come up. Willie was strangely listless and running a temperature of one hundred and one degrees. She began to worry, but remembered that pre-race nervousness can sometimes cause a horse's temperature to rise. The sweltering heat of the July evening wasn't helping either.

She decided to let Willie stand quietly in the cross-ties in his stall, then test his temperature again. A half-hour later, she withdrew the thermometer from his rectum for the second time and saw that his temperature was bordering on one hundred and two degrees. Alarmed, she scurried for help.

When Farrington heard of Willie's plight in the paddock, he swore softly, but immediately sought out the track veterinarian. The vet checked the colt and permitted Bob to scratch him, to remove him from the race.

His debut would have to be postponed.

Vivian and Seibert were sipping coffee in the handsome track restaurant, wondering why Bob had not brought Willie out for his warm-up miles, when they heard track announcer

Phil Georgeff's report. "Ladies and gentlemen, we have a late scratch in the third race. Scratch the four-horse, Rambling Willie."

"Damn," said Seibert, shaken. He immediately signaled the waitress for a check, commenting, "We better get down there and see what it's all about."

A small crowd had gathered outside Willie's stall by the time the two arrived. Farrington, Sandy, Al Bernard, and a couple of the stable's caretakers were milling about, talking quietly.

"Don't be upset, it's nothing but a touch of colt virus," Bob told his wife as she approached, concern on her face. "He's running a temp—Sandy caught it, thankfully—but he doesn't even have the sniffles. He'll be fine in a few days."

Al Bernard, knowing how much Vivian had looked forward to her horse's first start, was convinced she would be terribly disappointed, maybe shed a few tears. But Vivian surprised him, thanking Sandy for her diligence, and announcing placidly, "Well, we certainly don't want to start him if he's not a hundred percent."

Willie languished in his stall for a few days while the veterinarian and the stable crew treated him, then began to perk up. When his temperature had returned to normal and he grew feisty from boredom, Farrington directed Sandy to resume his jogging. Soon he was doing his best to run away on his female caretaker, and Farrington pronounced him cured.

This time the trainer chose a morning qualifying contest for the rebounding Willie. Jim Curran, bouncing back himself from his racing accident and anxious to resume his best driving year ever, took Willie to post in the practice dash and handled him carefully. Unraced since Ray Gibson had won with him at Anderson, Indiana, twenty-four days earlier, Willie loafed to a fourth-place finish, timed in 2:08 flat. Bob Farrington was satisfied.

An overabundance of horses in the cheaper classes at Maywood made it difficult to get Willie a race, but Farrington finally managed to land him one on August 13.

Vivian and Seibert, this time joined by Bob, were back at the clubhouse table as Willie and driver Curran were shuffled back to seventh for most of the race, then came with a big rush in the final quarter to finish second behind a victorious colt called Archibald.

The time for the race was a very fast 2:03 1/5, with Willie individually timed in 2:04 3/5. His performance was all the more impressive since he had been "parked out"—blocked from the rail and having to travel further than the horses inside him—for the last half of his journey. Since he was an unknown, the fans had sent him off as a nine-to-one longshot.

"No winner's circle picture tonight," Bob gently razzed his wife on the drive home. Considering the fact that Willie was her first horse, Vivian had told her husband that she would be content if he won but a single race—so that she could have her picture taken with him in the winner's circle.

"No, but he raced very well," Vivian said proudly.

"That he did. And he won you your first check, too," Bob reminded her. "You and Paul will be splitting $625. Not bad for a night's work."

"Oh, he'll win us a lot more than that. And I'll have that picture, too, before the season's over."

"I kinda think you will," Bob agreed, reaching over to squeeze his wife's hand.

But it wouldn't be right away. Maywood Park was closing, and the racing scene was shifting to Washington Park on the southwest fringe of Chicago. And Willie was still locked into one of the most heavily populated racing classifications at the new track—non-winners of $2,000. Races were hard to come by.

He did not start again until September 20, but the Farrington team had kept him fit and sharp. Once more he closed with a mighty rush to finish second in 2:03 3/5, only a single length behind the winner, Dancer's Image.

He was again wearing a controversial single shaft sulky, a homely, Rube Goldberg-looking contraption that resembled an auto exhaust system as its shaft rose from the horse's back and traveled on back to the driver's seat. Willie would wear the single shaft in all his races until the U.S. Trotting Association would ban it two years later. The unconventional sulky was said to provide freer movement for horses, making them faster. And Bob Farrington was for anything short of drugs to make his horses faster. Curran had driven him in his narrow loss to

Dancer's Image, but was hobbled again as Willie left the starting gate on October 5. But, then, Bob Farrington, like a kid eyeing his neighbor's new bicycle, had been aching to sit behind him in a race anyway.

Willie drew the one-post, the position nearest the rail, for the first time, meaning that he was not likely to be relegated to the rear of the pack, then have to make a big move in the late stages. Farrington settled him in the two-spot, tasting the leader's dust, and kept him there to the final turn for home. At that point, he steered him off the rail, hooted at him, rapped the saddle pad with his whip, and sat back to discover how Willie would respond.

The bay pacer was out and past the pacesetting horse in an instant, roaring down the stretch, building up lengths on the field as he went. At the wire, he had five full lengths on his rivals and had won in 2:03 1/5.

Vivian Farrington was too reserved to turn her emotions loose in the plush clubhouse, but Paul Seibert more than made up for her with a booming whoop of joy. Diners around them looked up in alarm, then smiled benevolently as Paul and Vivian embraced and made tracks for the escalator. Vivian's first horse had scored his first win for her, and she was determined to have her photo taken with him. The Red Man—her husband—grinned broadly as she burst into the winner's circle like a pink cyclone.

Farrington now knew he had a solid pacer in Willie, although he wasn't prepared to believe he had anything more than a decent claiming horse until the pair went back to the racing wars on October 13. In that event, Willie dawdled in fifth place to the three-quarter pole before unleashing his stretch kick. He flew past the four horses ahead and drew away to a seven-length triumph.

Bob glanced at the electronic timer as they flashed under the wire and did a double take. On a crisp autumn evening, with the cool temperature slowing the racing surface, Willie had paced his winning mile in 1:59 4/5! Breaking the two-minute barrier—the equivalent of a four-minute mile by a human—was one thing; accomplishing it on a cold evening in but his fourth pari-mutuel start was quite another.

Bob Farrington was reasonably certain at that moment that Rambling Willie would never have to face the indignity of competing in a claiming event, where a flock of eligible horsemen would be able to purchase him by merely posting his claiming price with the judges before the race.

Neither the Farringtons nor Seibert were live-it-up party-type folks, but a couple of bottles of champagne were opened when the three assembled back at the Dixie-Governor Motel near Washington Park later that night. No one realized it, but a tradition had started. All of Willie's great victories would be celebrated with the pop of corks.

And the Willie team, then and there, would have done itself a big favor by investing in a vineyard.

Paul Seibert was tired, a touch tipsy, and sublimely happy when he settled into bed. The Cincinnatian had never owned a two-minute horse before. In 1973, before the explosion of miracle miles a few years later, few had.

With a long day and exciting night behind him, his body yearned for sleep, but his restless mind fought it. For the first time—but certainly not the last—he was wrestling with a sort of perverted sense of guilt because his name was on Rambling Willie's registration papers. By all that was fair, Lloyd Arnold's name should have been on the papers. Arnold should be Vivian Farrington's partner on Willie.

Seibert knew how Vivian would explain it . . . how she would send the guilt feeling on its way. "Paul," she would say, "the Lord didn't mean for Lloyd to have Rambling Willie. He meant for you to have him."

Easy for Viv with her faith, Seibert mused. "But too damn complicated for me," he said aloud, with only a mattress, a few pieces of motel furniture, and a television set that didn't work for an audience.

Then he fell asleep.

Seibert had to watch Rambling Willie's next start alone. Bob and Vivian were on the West Coast racing the stable's aged pacing star, Shad Hanover, in a major stake at Hollywood Park in Inglewood, California. With Jim Curran reinjured, Bob had to drive, and he wasn't happy about it. He considered himself retired from driving, and wouldn't have steered Willie the second time if his son-in-law had been healthy.

The Red Man, who had been the nation's best only a few years back, was convinced that he couldn't do justice to Shad Hanover and Willie. He was sure he was too rusty, too old, and too heavy to give them the kind of drives they deserved. He drove now only because he had to.

Given a choice, Vivian Farrington would have been back in Chicago, rooting for Rambling Willie. But Bob liked his wife at his side. Normally, it worked both ways. Still, with Willie racing . . .

She had to be satisfied with a phone call back to Washington Park. Bob had already raced Shad Hanover, rust, age and weight notwithstanding, by the time she reached Paul Seibert. And Seibert was bubbling. With Joe Marsh, Jr., driving, the son of Rambling Fury had run off and hid on his foes again, winning by another seven open lengths.

"And the time?" Vivian pressed. "How fast did he go?"

"Depends on who you listen to," Mr. Seibert answered cryptically.

"What in the world does that mean?"

"It means the automatic timer went on the fritz at the half. The judges, timing by hand, gave him an official 2:00 4/5. But Marsh swears he caught him in 1:59 flat on his watch. Said he got him in twenty-seven seconds coming the final quarter. Called him the 'best damn green horse' he ever sat behind. What do you say about that, partner?"

"I say I'd better tell my husband, 'cause he's about to bust a blood vessel waiting to hear how our new *claimer* made out."

Rambling Willie raced twice more in 1973 before his trainer and owners brought his season to a close. Jim Curran, back in the bike again, steered him to cake-walking victories in 2:02 2/5 and 2:02 4/5, giving him a seasonal record of six wins and three seconds to show for his nine starts. His earnings totaled $9,524 for the year.

If Willie had been the average horse, the best years of his racing life would have been over, the peak of his earning power past. For in harness racing, the best is—and always has been—reserved for the young. For the two and three-year-old stakes colts, who travel from track to track and compete for purses that in 1980 ranged as high as $2,000,000 for a single race.

No harness horse in North America had ever reached a million dollars in earnings without having gained a large chunk of it in stakes for the young. And by 1973, only four American horses had reached that milestone by any means, under any circumstances.

The average horse, four years and up, has to scratch to pay his way, has to charge away from the gate week after week after week to make it worthwhile for his owner to keep him at the races. Rambling Willie would be turning four on January 1, the universal birthday for all horses.

But Willie was hardly the average horse.

Chapter 8

Good but not *great* things were expected of Rambling Willie as Bob Farrington began to train him back into shape for the 1974 racing season.

Sure, Vivian Farrington put his picture on her Christmas cards for 1973, although that was hardly unusual.

Harness racing people rarely convey their holiday wishes on conventional cards bearing the likenesses of Baby Jesus, Santa Claus, angels, choirs, snowmen, birds or churches. Chances are, you'll get a seasonal greeting from the trotting or pacing star of the stable—"Merry Christmas from Amber's Best" . . . "Happy Holidays from Briarwood Ed" . . . "Peace and Joy from Zelda Hanover."

And sometimes you get the horse's win record, too, so that hopes for a happy holiday and joyous new year are not simply arriving from plain, old Amber's Best, but from Amber's Best, 2:03 2/5.

Willie's 1973 mark—1:59 4/5—was on Vivian's cards, and, while no one in Willie's corner was looking for a magnificent new year, all were agreed that the record was liable to change for the better before Vivian got around to designing her Yule cards for 1974.

One night, sitting before a cozy, dancing blaze in the fireplace in the giant family room of the Farringtons' Richwood farmhouse, Bob reached over, tapped Paul Seibert on the knee, and asked, "What do you think your share of Willie's earnings will amount to in 1974?"

Seibert pondered the question for a moment, then responded thoughtfully, "I'd say, if everything goes right, he ought to win me something around $25,000.''

Farrington smiled. "I'll write you a check for that figure right now if you let me have whatever he makes beyond that," he offered.

"You think he might be that good?" Seibert said, surprised.

"I don't think he's a champion, or even a great horse," the trainer commented. "But I believe he's got the potential to earn $100,000 on the season."

"I'll drink to that," Seibert said happily, saluting Farrington with his glass.

Not that there hadn't been problems with Willie between the 1973 and 1974 racing seasons.

Willie had seemed a bit ouchy, hurting a little somewhere, in his last two starts in 1973, so Bob had ordered a nose to tail examination. Dr. Jim Kantzer, an Ohio-based veterinarian, confirmed what the trainer had suspected, a popped splint on the left front leg and a slight curb on the right rear. Both injuries were common to young horses, caused by the stress of racing, and generally not serious. Willie had responded swiftly after treatment.

Then the young horse had suffered a mild trauma of another type when his beloved caretaker, Sandy Smith, announced that she was leaving the world of standardbred horses to resume her college career.

Sandy had done an exceptional job with Willie, everyone agreed. Al Bernard was especially impressed with her work, claiming that the young woman had somehow imparted a sense of "manhood" to the neutered Willie. Bernard believed that gelded horses, in some curious manner, knew that some important function had been stolen from them and needed special attention, special treatment, to compensate for that loss. Sandy Smith had provided that extra devotion, Bernard felt.

Before she left the Richwood farm, where Willie was wintering, Sandy tried to persuade Bob's niece, Rhonda Farrington, to seek the job of caring for the pacer. But Rhonda, the teen-age daughter of Rod Farrington, was wary of the assignment.

"Sandy, I'd love to be Willie's groom," she pointed out. "But he's Aunt Vivian's first and only horse, and I'd never feel comfortable grooming him. I'd be afraid to leave his side for an instant, scared that something might happen to him while I was gone."

Rhonda, a small, very pretty girl, was already a caretaker with the Farrington aggregation, stationed, at the moment, with her horse at the Richwood headquarters. She was well aware that Sandy had survived just such an emergency a couple of weeks earlier. Sandy and Vivian had gone to the barn to visit Willie and found him choking on a knot of hay lodged in his throat. Bob had heard their screams and come running, roughly sticking a hand in the horse's throat to remove the blockage.

Rhonda Farrington could only imagine what would have happened had the two women not decided to visit Willie.

Sandy Smith's farewell was both traumatic and tearful, if a bit one-sided. Rambling Willie was accustomed to Sandy's bear hugs, had come to expect them. Her wracking sobs were rather new to him, however.

The search for Sandy's successor had to be swift. And was. Bob, talking the situation over with Viv and Seibert, settled quickly upon Mike Martin, a tall, handsome, kind of dreamy young man who had been with the stable for some time and had proven his ability and ambition on other Farrington horses. Possessing a sort of casual, cavalier attitude, it didn't bother Martin in the least that Willie was the property of the wife of the stable boss.

Mike, the son of horse people, struck an immediate rapport with his new pacer. Willie was the only horse detailed to him, meaning they were together constantly. Before long Willie would follow Martin like a faithful puppy without benefit of a lead shank.

Mike complained that Sandy Smith had utterly spoiled Willie with her constant mothering and her gifts of candy and fruit. Then Martin proceeded to do exactly the same thing, adding carrots, artichokes and other treats to Willie's menu. He offered Willie Coca Cola and beer, too, but found the bay horse preferred his bucket of fresh water to the more exotic drinks.

"Willie thinks he's a king," Martin told a fellow Farrington caretaker.

"Well, he ain't raced like it yet," the groom countered.

"He will. He will," Mike answered firmly.

Trainer Farrington and owners Paul Seibert and Vivian

were delighted with their selection of Martin. Willie was getting exactly the brand of day-to-day management they had come to expect from Sandy Smith. If anything, Mike was more loyal and ardent than his predecessor. While Vivian's and Paul's names might be on his registration, Mike grew to think of Willie as *his* horse. That fact would eventually lead to some bitter skirmishes between trainer and caretaker.

Those battles were well in the future, however, and as 1973 faded away and 1974 appeared, Bob Farrington was a contented man until he suffered a heavy personal blow. Louie Farrington, the patriarch of the Farrington racing clan, died of cancer in a Kenton, Ohio, hospital.

The Farrington standardbred empire reeled under the weight of the tragedy. Bob Farrington had always been the front man, the visual man, in the booming Farrington operation. But it had been Louie Farrington, toiling away backstage, who was responsible for making the empire purr along on eight cylinders. In such a simple matter as firing a recalcitrant caretaker, Louie had been the man. Bob ran the Chicago-based outfit, but he was far too soft-hearted to can anyone. Rough and gruff Louie had to drive up from Richwood to handle the deed.

The survivors—Bob, Dick, Rod and Brad Farrington—picked up the pieces and went on, but the mighty Farrington Stable that had ruled the Chicago racing scene for so many years would never be the same.

It was a saddened, solemn Bob Farrington who legged up Rambling Willie on the half-mile farm track at Richwood, then put him on a van for shipment up to Hawthorne Race Course on the western edge of the Windy City. The final touches, the spit and polish, would be applied to him there in preparation for his 1974 racing debut.

As Bob sat in the jog cart behind Willie, slowly circling first the farm track and then the Hawthorne oval, he couldn't help but think that his father would never have the opportunity of seeing Willie in action. They—Bob and Louie—had talked a great deal about Willie in those final days of the senior Farrington's life. Louie was extremely proud of his famous son and had immense faith in his ability to spot and develop a promising horse. And Bob had left little doubt that he thought he had a good one in Willie.

Bob's friends—Walt Paisley, Joe Marsh, Jr., Harry Burright, fellow horsemen like that—noticed the change in Farrington as they all assembled for the start of the new racing campaign. As quiet and reserved as he always seemed, Bob had forever been a man with a sly sense of humor and an appreciation of a good practical joke.

Paisley suffered from mixed emotions when he remembered how Farrington would roar past him in a race. Farrington and his horse would range up beside Paisley and his entry, then park there for a split second. Bob, rather casually, would look over at his rival and say, "See you back in the paddock, Kid." Then he would sting his horse once with the whip and pull away.

Marsh and Burright were fond of recalling what Bob had done to an inexperienced and nervous driver named Tommy Ryan. Ryan, for some reason, was unable to make the chirping noise that horsemen use as a signal to get their horses into high gear. Instead, Ryan carried a small bird whistle that fitted snugly between the top of his tongue and the roof of his mouth. When Ryan wanted a maximum effort from his horse, he'd blow the whistle.

Farrington thought it hilarious and resolved to do something about it the first time he found himself in a race with Ryan. When it finally happened, Bob spent the better part of a race mile trying to shake up his friendly rival. At the three-quarter pole, parked outside his nervous adversary and screaming dire warnings of impending disaster, Farrington managed to succeed with his mission. Ryan swallowed the whistle.

But there was little humor in Robert Farrington as he checked into Hawthorne in February and promptly reaffirmed that son-in-law Jim Curran would again handle all Farrington Stable driving assignments during the year, including Rambling Willie. Bob himself would drive only in cases of extreme emergency, and perhaps not at all, he said.

"I had an idea he might try a comeback this year," Walt Paisley told a newsman. "But he's dead serious. It's the end of an era."

Farrington and his owners like Lloyd Arnold and Paul Seibert were satisfied that Curran would continue to do an excellent job with the stable's horses. Curran had driven most of them in 1973 and had harvested $828,433 in racing purses, despite a racing injury that had kept him idle for nearly two months.

Jim Curran, a quiet, good looking, thirty-year old, was a third generation harness horseman, who had arrived on the Chicago circuit after a solid and sound apprenticeship at the racetracks in Michigan. After a long courtship, he had married Bob and Vivian Farrington's daughter, Karen Sue, in 1971, and started to drive the Farrington horses a year later when Bob refractured his shoulder at Sportsman's Park and informed the racing world that he was slipping into semi-retirement.

Bob and his lieutenants, Al "Cat" Bernard, and brother Dick Farrington, would get the horses ready; Jim Curran would drive them. And, when Curran was unavailable, or when a conflict cropped up, Dick Farrington would fill in. Bob would watch the action from a seat in the clubhouse or grandstand.

With that resolution duly announced, Farrington immediately shattered it, reporting that he would drive Rambling Willie in Willie's first start of the year. "I want to make certain he goes an easy trip after the layoff," he explained.

Willie went back to the races on February 25. He was officially four years old, was a shade taller than when he'd quit the track three months earlier, and was carrying some sixty or seventy more pounds on his long frame.

The American harness horse normally arrives at his physical peak between the ages of four and six, then begins an inevitable slide downhill that eventually results in his retirement from racing. Some standardbreds reach their zenith as early as three years and are well along the downward trail at four. Others mature later or keep their racing edge longer. Bob Farrington suspected—certainly hoped—that Willie belonged to the latter class, that he would continue to blossom in 1974, then retain that sharpness for one, two, or even three more years.

But only time would tell.

Willie left from the four-post on a bitterly cold evening, an occasional snowflake dipping and diving past the big track lights as he rolled along. Farrington raced him very carefully, never asking him for real speed, never getting after him. Still, with his patented stretch charge in fine working order, he made up three full lengths in the drive to come within a neck of the leader at the wire. It was an excellent performance in a relatively easy race, exactly what Farrington was looking for in Willie's return to competition.

"I got him nice and tight for you, and he's all yours the rest of the way," he told Curran in the paddock.

Eleven nights later Curran nursed him away from the ten-post, got snarled in heavy traffic, and had to race him on the outside the entire mile. But Willie still had zip enough to collar the pacesetter in the drive, scoring a one-length victory in 2:05.

A week later he was short by a neck again, racing over a muddy track, but returned the following week to win handily by four lengths in 2:04.

"He's some kind of nice pacer," Curran commented to Vivian as the Farringtons and the Currans stopped for coffee after the race.

"Of course he is," Vivian agreed readily. "He's my boy, and he's going to be a champion."

"Well," Curran hedged, unprepared to go that far.

Most of Willie's early success had come in the Suburban Downs Pacing Series, with the purse climbing with every start. Where he had opened the season in a simple conditioned race bearing a $5,000 purse, his latest triumph had come in a series leg offering an $11,250 prize—fifty percent of it earmarked for the winner.

But the increasing prosperity also meant that his competition was getting stiffer, tougher with every outing. Not only was he racing against some of the best young horses in the Chicago area, but against a number of rugged old veterans as well. The kind that Bob Farrington hoped Willie would evolve into. Journeymen pacers who might have lost a step or two of speed over the years, but made up for it with racing guile picked up over those same years.

Willie faced his sternest test—and his largest purse by far—in his fifth race of the year. He had easily qualified for the $40,000 final leg of the Suburban Series; was one of the co-favorites, in fact. Rin Tim Tim, a three-year-old who had yet to taste defeat in 1974, was the other. Nine additional survivors of the series merely filled out the rest of the bulky field in the eyes of the 13,291 fans turning out for the stakes contest.

The Farringtons, sensing victory, were all decked out in

their finest finery, Bob's ensemble having been hand-picked as usual by his wife. Paul Seibert, sniffing victory, too, had even consented to wearing a necktie in honor of the occasion.

But the Willie team might just as well have worn blue jeans.

With a kind of half rain, half snow falling, and a sticky, muddy track underfoot, Rambling Willie, in the most important event of his young career, went the worst mile of his young career. He was never a factor in the stake. Willie was third at the quarter, sixth at the half, *eighth* at the three quarters, and rallied to be sixth at the finish—eleven discouraging lengths behind the victorious Rin Tim Tim.

Rin Tim Tim's owners, prancing about the soggy winner's circle, were beside themselves with glee.

Rambling Willie's owners were in shock.

"Bob, I don't know what the hell was wrong with him," a disconsolate, mud-splattered Jim Curran reported. "I got after him real good, but he had no pace, no lick, no wallop whatsoever. None at all."

"He looked sound," Farrington ventured.

"Sound's a dollar," Curran confirmed.

"He's not showing any fever. No runny nose . . ."

"None of those things."

"He's raced in the slop before."

"Never seemed to bother him in the past."

"Maybe . . ." said Farrington thoughtfully, "he just plain went a bad race. In that case, we'll simply have to wait 'til next time."

"Don't tell Viv," Curran offered confidentially, "but bad race or good, I don't think Willie's ever going to beat that Rin Tim Tim colt."

Farrington stared at his son-in-law for a long moment. Then he said softly, "Yes he will. He'll beat him."

A week later—on April 6—four-year-old Willie and three-year-old Rin Tim Tim met for the second time. It was a basic overnight event, with only a pedestrian purse of $6,400 offered, although Farrington had trained and honed his horse as though the prize were ten times that sum. Rin Tim Tim was the first of the great young horses that would sprout in Willie's path year after year. Farrington thought it imperative that his horse beat the youngster if Willie were to become a first class racehorse.

The Hawthorne crowd left little doubt concerning the way it felt about the two. Its dollars poured through the pari-mutuel machines to make Rin Tim Tim a three-to-five favorite in the six-horse race. Willie, coming off his incredibly poor performance in the Suburban finale, was a decided longshot at eight-to-one odds.

Paul Seibert, secretly sharing Jim Curran's opinion that Willie was not likely to whip his younger rival, became even gloomier as he watched the field assemble behind the starting gate. Paul had decided to view the race from the grandstand apron, the black-topped area between the stands and the track fence. Glancing over at the winner's circle, he spotted Rin Tim Tim's owners poised near the entrance to the charmed area. It was obvious they had gathered to have their photo taken as soon as the test was over. Paul couldn't blame them.

"Aannnd they're off," track announcer Phil Georgeff drawled dramatically to send the field on its way.

Rambling Willie looked ominously like the Rambling Willie of a week earlier in the early stages. He left the gate slowly and settled in fifth while his flashy young rival moved immediately to the top. Willie was still fifth at the half, and pacing lacklusterly along in the same position at the three-quarters. Half embarrassed and with a hint of sadness, Paul Seibert pulled his eyes off the field and focused them on the dark asphalt at his feet.

"*Coming off the turn and straightening out for home, it's Rin Tim Tim, pacing easily, leading by two,*" race-caller Georgeff reported in sing-song fashion. "*But here comes Gulliver off the rail and taking up the chase,*" he added in a new tempo. "*And on the far outside, it's Rambling Willie beginning to move.*"

Seibert's glance returned to the field. Halfway down the stretch, Rin Tim Tim was still on top, but Gulliver was inching up, closing the gap. And, wondrously, Paul could see Jim Curran's gray and gold colors growing larger, more vivid, with every step. Rambling Willie was flying, now fourth, now third, now about to overhaul the charging Gulliver in second.

The frenzied noise a crowd creates when the finish of a race is to be a cliff-hanger was nothing new to Paul Seibert;

he'd heard it a thousand times over the years. But he'd never quite heard the strange, undulating, collective shriek splitting the night air at Hawthorne. It was half a chant, half a scream, with a shrill "eeee" at the end of it. His eyes were now riveted on the race, but his mind was straining to identify the sound, to understand the wild message.

Then it hit him. The throng, or at least a healthy portion of it, was screaming, "Will-eeee! Will-eeee! Will-eeee!"

The crowd was pleading for his horse.

Seibert sucked up a chest full of air, held it, and watched Rambling Willie thunder past the wire. Paul did not wait for the photo sign to come down, but headed for the winner's circle. He knew Bob and Vivian Farrington would be meeting him there.

Chapter 9

*I*t was clearly a blessing, the Reverend C. Lloyd Harris decided, to be back out on the sun porch, the windows open, the warm and brilliant rays of sunshine warming his face, making him squint, a tender and fragrant May breeze mildly ruffling his hair.

The porch was Reverend Harris' favorite place to work and reflect, and that was why his cherished rolltop desk, the one he had paid five dollars for in 1926, was located there. Of course, the porch was no place to be when the winter winds ripped across the flatlands of Central Ohio, but they were gone now. It was May 10, 1974, and the Lord had served up a day that made it difficult to remember the cold and ice and snow of the recently perished winter.

Harris was working on his Sunday sermon, although "tinkering" might be more accurate, he had to admit. The sermon was finished, and the polish he was applying to it was more an excuse to enjoy the clear and balmy morning than it was to improve the quality of his message to the parishioners of the West Mansfield Church of Christ.

Lloyd Harris was not in the habit of deceiving himself, and made little effort to do so now. What he had, he admitted, was a case of spring fever, the same malady that was doubtless afflicting school children all over Central Ohio . . . in every area penetrated by the glorious morning.

Curiously, or maybe it was a blessing too, he had little or nothing to do that day. He was still working three afternoons a week at the J and J Market across the street, but this day wasn't one of them. His sermon, quite frankly, was completed. He knew of no ailing parishioners that needed cheering up, and, thankfully, no wedding rehearsal was scheduled that evening. The wedding business, he knew, would soar the next month—June.

As he leaned back in his swivel chair—like the desk, an antique—he could hear his wife rustling about upstairs, beginning her day. Bonnie Harris had never shared her husband's penchant for early rising, which was perfectly all right with the reverend. The Harrises had never eaten breakfast—it was a sort of ritual of denial—so there was little reason for her to rise at dawn after all the children had grown and left to create families of their own.

Nevertheless, Harris would welcome her presence this morning, as he did every morning. After nearly a half-century of marriage, Bonnie Harris was still good company.

"Lloyd, are you out on the porch?" Mrs. Harris asked as she descended the stairs.

"Yes, Mother. Out here enjoying the beautiful day that God has given us, trying to think of something worthwhile to occupy my day. Or, at least, to keep me busy until the mail comes."

"Did you ever consider relaxing?" Bonnie Harris inquired.

"Now, Mother . . ." Harris sputtered. ". . . I'm sure the Lord meant for us to keep busy."

"Then why would He create a lovely day like this and arrange it so that you have little to do?"

"Probably challenging me to find something," Harris answered instantly.

It was a losing battle, Mrs. Harris decided.

"How about the flowers, Mother?" her husband pressed. "Is it too early to plant them?"

"No, Lloyd," she said resignedly. "If that's what you'd like to do, it's all right. But don't forget to water them good," she added lightly.

"Ha," the reverend said.

It was a family joke, the flowers. The Harrises, generally pressed for time, had long given up the practice of planting and nurturing flowers around the base of their home. Instead, they'd bought a profusion of plastic flowers, literally hundreds of them. Each spring, the reverend would haul them out of the cellar and "plant them," sticking their plastic covered wire bases into the ground. Later, Mrs. Harris would go out and improve the "arrangement." In the autumn, both would pluck them out of the ground, wrap them carefully in newspapers, and cart them back into the basement for "replanting" the next spring.

Lloyd Harris was aware the flowers looked artificial at close range, but from the street they appeared real, lending a colorful touch to the two-story, white framed home. And they saved a great deal of wear and tear on his aged, stooped back. The necessity for weeding was minimal.

"Planting" the flowers was a task that he enjoyed. He felt he was accomplishing something worthwhile—adding a splash of color to the world—yet his mind was left unoccupied, free to roam to subjects of his choosing. And on this strikingly handsome May morning, he discovered, he chose to think of his daughter, Vivian, and her harness racing husband, Bob Farrington.

He hadn't heard from Vivy lately, and that disturbed him. When he'd last seen Vivian and Bob, both had been downhearted, still depressed by the death of Bob's father, Louis Farrington. While death did not affect Lloyd Harris so profoundly—as a totally believing man of God, he saw death as a beautiful beginning, not an unhappy ending—he was aware that everyone did not benefit from that insight. Bob Farrington had been shattered by his father's death, and his gloom and depression had spread to Vivian.

Lloyd Harris had liked Louie Farrington, although they had little in common other than the bond created by the marriage of their children. Louis Farrington was a rough-hewn man, given to using tough language that was sometimes an affront to Reverend Harris' ear. Yet, Louis had been a Christian, had supported the church when it was possible, and his mother had taught Sunday School for many, many years. There was never a doubt that Louis Farrington had been anything but a warm and loving father-in-law to Vivian.

Harris was even more fond of Louie Farrington's youngest son, Bob, Vivian's husband. Oh, he—Harris—had been against their marriage at the time, but Vivian had been only a junior in high school, seemingly far too young to marry. And, of course, the reverend had held some serious reservations about Bob's choice of careers; he had, in fact, been sure that

Bob and Vivian would end up destitute as Bob tried to make a living training and driving horses.

But he'd been gloriously wrong on both counts, he admitted for perhaps the hundredth time. The union of Vivian and Bob had been a continuing success, almost as though the match had been made, well, in Heaven. And who could question the sparkling record that Bob had rung up in racing, winning the national driving championship so many times?

And Bob Farrington was considerably more than just a fine husband and an ultra-successful horseman. He was religious, too, a Christian, in his own way. Reverend Harris could well remember the Sunday—it was, in fact, one of his fondest recollections—when Bob had accepted Jesus Christ as his Savior. His action had been totally unexpected, surprising not only his own family, but everyone in the congregation that day. Bob's coming forward had brought a mist to every eye in the church, Reverend Harris' certainly included.

Harris, plunging the last of the plastic flowers into the dirt base that rimmed the house, said a silent prayer for his son-in-law, asking the Lord to ease his grief, to give Bob something to help him forget the loss of his father.

Harris was standing back, admiring his work, when Bonnie Harris announced through an open window that it was lunch time. Spryly, the eighty-two year-old pastor rounded the house, climbed the back steps, and headed for the kitchen sink to wash his hands after his hour and a half of "gardening."

"What are your plans this afternoon, Lloyd?" his wife inquired as they finished their tuna salad sandwiches.

"I don't rightly know," he responded. "I'll check the mail," he added. "Might be something interesting there. Maybe some orders for the salve. Something like that."

"You ought to plan a nap," his wife advised. "Since you've got the time for a change."

"Naps are for old people," he commented, meaning it.

"Not young fellas like you?"

"No. I'll get the mail. Need anything at the store?"

"Not a thing," she said, unwilling to give him the slightest reason to stop in the J and J Market, where, unless young manager Jim Goodwin was there to shoo him out, he'd surely begin to stock the shelves or bag groceries.

"Just the mail, then," he announced over his shoulder.

Once out of the house and onto the sidewalk, he made a conscious effort to slow his gait. The day was far too beautiful to hurry. It was meant to be savored. He reached the corner, crossed the street and passed the market where he worked part-time. He knew there would be few real shoppers in the store at this hour, mostly children buying cupcakes or candy. He had no urge to pop inside to see what was happening, but knew himself well enough to realize that he might do just that on the return trip if nothing of any consequence or interest appeared in his postal box.

Happily, he noticed the box contained several envelopes, some of them genuine-looking letters and not merely advertisements. In his anxiety, he erred in working the combination to the box and had to start over. Soon the day's delivery was in his hands and he was checking the envelopes. The first was from a customer, one of the dozens of folks from several states who bought his Balm of Gilead, the healing salve he concocted and sold. The second was from the telephone company, obviously his monthly bill. And then he spotted the familiar handwriting of his daughter, Vivian, and he felt an immediate bolt of warmth in his chest.

The reverend was tempted to open the letter there in the post office, more a storefront than an actual building designed for the collection and distribution of mail. But he thought better of it. It was his habit to open all mail at his rolltop desk—when weather permitted—and the practice was too much a part of him to change at this late date. Besides, like the weather, he would be able to savor the letter on the way home. And give him a chance to pray that it contained good news, possibly word that Bob had escaped from his melancholy. Harris walked past the grocery store at a rapid clip and never gave it a thought.

He was back on the sun porch, ensconced in his well worn chair, facing his beloved desk, when he opened the letter. As he tore open the envelope, a small slip of paper floated to the floor, but he ignored it in his haste to reach his daughter's words. He read them slowly, carefully. Then uncharacteristically, he bellowed, "Mother, come here quick!"

"Lloyd, what's wrong!?" his wife demanded, arriving on the porch at a jog.

"Letter from Vivy," he said by way of explanation.

"With bad news?" she asked. "Why in the world did she wait to write? Why didn't she phone? What's wrong?"

"Wrong? Nothing. Nothing's wrong. Quite the opposite. Good news. Great news! Here, read," he said, pushing the note into her hands.

Mrs. Harris pulled a pair of steel-rimmed glasses from her apron pocket, unfolded them, placed them on her nose, and read:

Dearest Dad—

Enclosed is a check for $1,465. It is my latest tithe from Rambling Willie's earnings. Willie has only started six times this year, but has already earned $29,312. He is truly an amazing horse, and Bob believes he will win $100,000 before the year is over.

Willie has been a Godsend to us. He has lifted Bob out of the grief caused by his father's death. He has made life very exciting for Paul Seibert and myself. And now, hopefully, he will be able to truly help God and your church.

Dad, I know you're going to fight me on this, but I want you to take $650 from the check and buy that modern church sign that you've been talking about for so long . . . the one you saw at the convention. That's a must. Orders from headquarters.

Mom, you see that he buys it.

Got to run now. Be calling you one of these nights.

All My Love,
Vivian

"Why, that's wonderful, Lloyd," Mrs. Harris commented as the reverend retrieved the check from the floor, then stared at it.

"It is," he said with reverence. "She told me she was going to tithe that horse's earnings, and she sent me a small check at the end of the year. But I never expected anything like this. That's a lot of money . . . ."

"And a lot more to come, if what Bob seems to believe comes to pass," she pointed out.

"That's true," he agreed.

"And now, at long last, you can order your sign . . . ."

"Oh, no," he interrupted.

"What?"

"I can't order the bulletin board. It's just too . . . well . . . it's too extravagant."

"Lloyd Harris," his wife said sternly, "your daughter directed you to buy the sign. After all, it's her money to spend as she sees fit. If someone else in the church tithed their money, but told you what to spend it on, what would you do?"

"Spend it as they requested," he admitted.

"Well, then, should your daughter expect anything less? Should she be treated any differently?" his wife pressed.

"I suppose not," he said.

Then he beamed. "It's a beautiful board. Big letters, easy to read. Nice and sturdy. And did I tell you, it lights up at night?"

"Many times," said Mrs. Harris. "Many times."

"But it's not going to be easy," he added, his mood changing again.

"What's that?"

"Telling the board I'm going to buy a $650 sign for the outside of the church. And telling them the money came from a racehorse."

"From what Vivy says, they'd better get used to the idea," Mrs. Harris said matter-of-factly.

Chapter 10

*I*t wasn't that Helen Farrington, Bob's aunt, had never heard people talking to horses; she was a Farrington, completely immersed in harness racing, prepared to believe anything of horse owners. It was simply that she'd never noticed a horse "talking back" before.

"Are you going to win tonight, Willie?" Vivian Farrington was inquiring of her pacer, while Aunt Helen, a patronizing expression decorating her face, looked on.

Rambling Willie's long head, sticking out the door of his stall on the Maywood Park backstretch, shook vigorously from side to side.

"No? You're not? What's the matter," chided Vivian, "are you afraid of Braidwood?"

Willie looked hard at his owner. Then his head plunged up and down.

"You're being very silly," Vivian scolded. "I'm sure you can beat him if you set your mind to it."

Without hesitation, Willie's head began to shake from side to side again.

"Vivian," Helen Farrington interrupted, the skepticism beginning to give way to wonder, "do you often talk to Willie that way?"

"Quite often," said Vivian.

"And does he answer you?"

"Always."

"And you ask him if he's going to win?"

"Sometimes. Generally when I think he's got a chance. He confirms it for me. Or tells me he's not."

"And is he accurate?"

"Usually. Oh, once in a while he tells me he's going to win and he doesn't. But that's because he gets caught in traffic. Or maybe the race doesn't unfold the way it should. Something like that. On the whole, he's pretty accurate."

"But tonight he doesn't stand a chance . . . ?"

"None at all. You saw him. He's intimidated by Braidwood, and he won't be beating him until he gets it clear in his mind that he can."

"I see," said Helen Farrington.

And, strangely, she almost did. Helen, sister of the late Louie Farrington, and a sort of unofficial chronicler of the Farrington family's racing history, had known Vivian for more than thirty years. Knew her to be a fine wife, great mother, and a person with a level head on her shoulders. Knew her to be deeply religious, but not the kind of fanatic who hustled about foisting it upon others.

Helen had also been hearing reports from reliable persons concerning the bizarre, almost mystical, relationship that had grown between Vivian and Rambling Willie. She had heard them from Bob Farrington. From Paul Seibert. From Al Bernard. From Mike Martin, Willie's proprietary groom.

Willie, they said, knew instantly when Vivian was in the area of the Farrington Stable. Willie, they said, was intensely jealous and would grow angry if Vivian stopped to greet another horse before appearing at his stall. Willie, they said, would bare his teeth if she arrived wearing fur. Willie, they said, would shun her if she showed up with anything but Norell perfume on. And Willie, they all said, would "talk" with Viv, would tell her when he felt he was going to win.

Helen Farrington may have been harboring lingering doubts when she and Vivian joined Bob and Paul Seibert at the clubhouse table, but she had to confess she couldn't bring herself to bet on Willie that night. Nor was she surprised when Willie, who was gunning for his fourth straight victory, finished fifth, three lengths back of the winner, *Braidwood*.

Eight nights later, back in Xenia, Ohio, where she was dean of women at the Ohio Soldiers and Sailors Orphans Home, Helen answered the phone to hear Vivian report that Willie had won at Maywood in 1:59 4/5, equaling his lifetime speed record.

"I take it Braidwood was racing elsewhere," Helen commented matter-of-factly.

"Of course," Vivian said.

Helen laughed.

"But we'll get him yet," Vivian promised. "It's a matter of me building up Willie's confidence."

"You'll do it, Viv."

"I know it."

By early August, with a little more than half the racing season over, Rambling Willie had not beaten Braidwood, but was sporting a creditable record. He'd raced twenty times, scoring eight wins, finishing second five times, and earning a little over $66,000. He'd lowered his win record to 1:59 flat and been photoed out in 1:58 4/5. A short bout with a virus had probably kept him from doing a shade better.

Trainer Bob Farrington was generally satisfied with the way he had raced. Farrington had predicted before the season that Willie would be a good racehorse, not a great one, and he had seen nothing to really change his mind.

Bob, for the most part, had shaken the melancholy left by his father's death, but was gearing up to face a calamity of another sort. Lloyd Arnold, his perennial horse partner, the mainstay of his stable, was planning to travel a new racing road. Arnold wanted to rid himself of all the racing stock he now owned—the claimers, the raceway veterans—and buy expensive yearling colts and fillies to race on the Grand Circuit.

Arnold had proven everything that he had set out to prove: that it was possible to make money racing horses if the person or persons involved went about it in a businesslike manner. Now he wanted a bigger challenge, the biggest challenge of them all in the racing game. He wanted to spend hundreds of thousands of dollars on fragile, risky, well-bred babies, hoping to get his money back in either the super-rich Grand Circuit stakes, or in the breeding business.

He was hankering to roll the dice in the chanciest of racing's crap games.

But he would have to do it without Bob Farrington. Farrington was wary from the start and grew less enthusiastic as his partner continued to outline his plans. Bob was a raceway trainer, the finest of them all for a long period, and had never campaigned on the Grand Circuit. He had tinkered with a few yearlings over his career, but had enjoyed little success with them. His *thing*, his father's *thing*, and Lloyd Arnold's *thing*, until now, had been to buy or claim ready-made horses, then improve on them.

Farrington, still a farm boy, a homebody at heart, was not fond of travel, and knew what the Grand Circuit schedule was like: Brandywine Raceway in Delaware one week, Wolverine Raceway in Detroit the next, Batavia Downs in New York the next. A week here, a week there, throughout the late spring, summer and autumn. And when you got a week off, it only meant your horses were lame or sick, which hardly made for a relaxing vacation.

If that weren't enough, Farrington was retired from driving, would only take twenty-four horses to post in 1974. And he sensed that his intense, aggressive partner had in mind a stable boss who would not only break and train his expensive youngsters, but drive them as well.

By late summer, Bob Farrington and Lloyd Arnold had agreed—mutually, amicably—to dissolve the powerful Farrington Stable-Arnold Cattle Company organization. Since all the horses were to be disposed of, they began to lower the claiming price on some of their joint stock, a sort of going-out-of-business clearance sale. Those that weren't lost through the claiming game—more than a hundred head—were consigned to the annual Tattersall's mixed auction in Lexington, Kentucky, in November.

Incredibly, the Farrington-Arnold partnership had gathered in some $7,000,000 in racing purses over its nine-year existence.

The sport buzzed over the breakup, serving up a dozen different, vicious, inaccurate reasons for the demise. In later years, some would say the parting of the ways came about because of Rambling Willie; that Farrington had ignored Arnold to give half the horse to Paul Seibert. But that was nonsense. Willie was nothing more than a promising claiming horse when Farrington bought him, nothing but a good, solid racehorse when their partnership ended. Not that Arnold did not take a shot—perhaps in jest—at buying Willie when the break came.

"He's not for sale, Lloyd," Farrington told him seriously, whether Arnold was kidding or not.

Dissolving the partnership was a jolt, a hurting thing to Robert Farrington. And the hurt only increased in magnitude when Dick Farrington, Bob's older brother, announced that he was leaving the Farrington family operation to handle the spanking new Lloyd Arnold Roarin' Grand stable. Richard, three years older than Bob, a talented horseman in his own right, could not resist the sparkling brass ring offered by the lanky Arnold. There was no question in Dick's mind—in anyone's mind—that Lloyd Arnold would go first class. Nor that he would succeed.

Robert Farrington did not resent his brother's defection. It simply saddened him. Bob, looking on as horse after horse was plucked away from him in claiming races, reviewed the year and retreated into a shell. He had lost his father, his partner, his brother, and his horses. He worked hard at hiding his depression when he was at the racetrack, but cronies like Paisley and Marsh, as always, could see through the veneer. And the people who knew him even better—Vivian, Seibert, Bernard, Aunt Helen—agonized for him, knowing the size of the ache he carried around with him.

Rambling Willie, at times, managed to pierce his gloom, to sprinkle a little sunshine in his life. At other times, he merely added to his collection of woes.

On August 16, Willie came within a whisker of defeating the mighty Braidwood, his current arch-rival, trained, driven and partially owned by a proud Walter Paisley. Eight nights later he was only a length short of Braidwood at the wire, closing from fifth at the top of the stretch, while his fans chanted the now familiar, "Will-eeee! Will-eeee!"

But then he turned in three lackluster performances in a row, winding up sixth, fourth, and then sixth again in races he should or could have won. On two of the occasions, he was favored. On the other, when he finished fourth, he was in and out of traffic the whole mile, and hardly in contention as Braidwood scored still another triumph for Paisley.

Farrington was tempted to call it a season with him after a desultory effort on September 13, when he finished another five lengths off the pace in a creaking mile that went in 2:01 2/5.

But he kept him at Washington Park, where the racing had shifted, and was rewarded with a 1:58 2/5 journey that netted him a dead heat for third in a photo finish that involved the first four horses across the wire.

Suddenly, dramatically, he was the darling of the fans once more, pumping life and adrenalin into a deflated Bob Farrington. He closed with a breathtaking rush to win in 1:59 1/5, then returned a week later to accomplish what he'd been unable to do most of the season; beat Braidwood.

Vivian Farrington had been ''chatting'' with him for weeks, trying by words, tone, osmosis, or whatever, to instill confidence in him. Willie had come perilously close to catching his tough contemporary in the two recent outings, but had fallen far short in their last encounter. This time—bolstered by Vivian's therapy or not—he insured the victory by pacing the last quarter in 27 seconds. Not even the sizzling Braidwood could withstand that kind of pressure.

It was like whipping Rin Tim Tim all over again, only better. As the Farringtons and ever-present partner Paul Seibert shared a magnum of champagne for the first time in weeks, Vivian hustled off to a phone booth to call Aunt Helen.

Willie's heroics continued the next week with a 1:59 2/5 score over a cast of six rivals that did not include Braidwood. But his effort inspired Mike Kiley of the Chicago *Tribune* to write of him in glowing terms.

''Rambling Willie's 11 season victories have mostly been the result of a final speed flash that should create quite a breeze for the railbirds by the finish line,'' Kiley wrote. ''His most recent decision was captured in a blistering last quarter of 27 3/5 seconds en route to a 1:59 2/5 mile.

''Often times thru-out the year—Rambling Willie's first full campaign after winning six of nine starts in 1973—the son of Rambling Fury-Meadow Belle has appeared to have little chance as late as midway in the stretch. However, with the power reminiscent of a Larry Csonka, he's exploded thru suddenly-opened holes to prevail, or displayed the sheer sprint speed of a Herb Washington to overcome the leader.''

But it was his last good press notice of the year. Just as rapidly as his late season spurt had begun, it ground to a halt. The withering ''kick'' the Kiley had described so graphically abruptly left him, and it was all downhill from there. In his next

four starts, he finished fourth, fourth, fourth and fifth, display-
ing lethargy in circling the big Washington Park racetrack. He
was just another horse filling out the field for the feature race.

On November 14, when he could come no closer than
eleven lengths of horses he would have thrashed a few weeks
earlier, a mystified, chastened, disappointed Bob Farrington
sent him home to the farm in Richwood.

Willie had ended the year with $98,488 in purses.

A good season, but hardly great.

Farrington, whose emotions and mental state had resembled a roller coaster from the start of the season, was down
again. Way down. As Willie was en route back to Richwood,
more than a hundred of the racehorses and broodmares he had
owned with Lloyd Arnold were under the auctioneer's gavel in
Lexington. Their sale would give Bob a sizeable bank balance,
but leave him practically bereft of horses. For all practical pur-
poses, he was starting from scratch.

He never complained as he puttered about the big farm, or
took short trips to check out horses that might fit into the new,
smaller Farrington stable. If he longed for the days when he
ruled the harness sport as its driving champion, or pined for
the period when he was maestro of one of the most powerful
racing organizations in the world, he never showed it.

But the pride was there, still sizzling away like the fireplace in his handsome family room. The Farrington clan and
friends like Paul Seibert knew that and did not need a sign to
confirm it. But they got it anyway. On a cold, blustery night in
December, Farrington announced, without fanfare, that he
would drive Rambling Willie throughout the balance of the
pacer's career.

Chapter 11

*R*acing harness horses at the Chicago area tracks has never been for the meek, the mild, the faint-hearted. The tracks themselves, and for the most part, the horsemen who have raced there, have been honorable and honest, providing quality racing, laced with integrity. But from the days of Al Capone to the present, there's been an outside criminal element that has constantly chipped away at Chicago racing, often leaving druggings, theft, arson and murder in its wake.

As recently as 1978, unknown parties, after two abortive attempts, managed to burn down Hawthorne Race Course. A year earlier, Washington Park had been a victim of fire, with arson a possible cause. That same year, hoodlums broke into the Sportsman's Park racing office, making off with the detailed racing records of eight hundred horses competing there. And still in 1977, trainer-driver Jim Wondergem was gunned to death in an incident occurring in Addison, Illinois.

That same aura of violence, of intrigue, of crime, was present when Bob Farrington, like a bandleader with a new group, sent his scaled-down, streamlined stable of racehorses up to Hawthorne to commence the 1975 season. The fifty-horse aggregation of past years was gone, but the twenty trotters and pacers he shipped to the Windy City were fresh, sharp and sound. Rounding them up, then training them into peak condition, had filled Bob with satisfaction and blown away the funk that had settled on him in 1974. The bounce was back in his stride, the grin back on his face, as he left Richwood in February.

"It's the soundest, best conditioned bunch I've had in years," he told Vivian. "We should do a whole lot of winning, at least in the early part of the season."

Jim Curran was still doing the bulk of the stable's driving, although Farrington, as he had proclaimed, was the man up behind Rambling Willie as the horses started going to post.

"He's going to be so good this year that he'll cover up my mistakes," he joked to Curran.

Willie opened the new campaign with a pair of decent efforts in invitational competition, finishing second and third, then scored a 2:01 2/5 triumph in his third trip away from the starting gate.

But, oddly, he was the only horse in the stable racing near his potential. The rest looked and acted good in the barn, but had no stamina, no staying power, in their races. They often left the gate with speed and strength, but straggled home, generally finishing out of the money.

Baffled, the Farrington crew trained them harder, longer, but to no avail. Then they backed them off, eased the training regimen, fearing they might be guilty of overtraining, of peaking the horses too soon. Still they finished up the racetrack, out of the money.

Every horse in the barn was checked for virus, but no hint of that fast spreading malady could be found. Temperatures were normal, and there wasn't an unsound animal in the collection.

"What the hell's wrong with 'em?" Cat Bernard demanded of his boss. "We had 'em razor sharp when we left Richwood."

"Damned if I know, but I'm getting suspicious," Farrington said grimly. "Joe Marsh says he's got the same problem; a stable full of horses that look like a million, but race like a nickel."

"My God, you don't think they're drugged, do you?"

"I sure as hell hope not, but I think it's time we looked into that possibility."

Two days later—on a Sunday—an Ohio veterinarian was flown in, taking blood and fecal samples from every horse in the Farrington Stable. Two weeks later, the vet reported that he had found traces of a tranquilizing drug in every horse, the livers of each enlarged from an apparent steady dose of the offending chemical. The least affected—the healthiest of the bunch—was Rambling Willie.

"Why would Willie be any different?" Farrington asked.

"Hard to say," the vet said. "The drug was apparently fed them through their food. Or maybe in their water. Was Willie's diet any different than the rest?"

"I don't think so," Farrington answered slowly.

"Is he fed anything the others don't get?"

"Not really. Outside of the brown sugar Viv feeds him."

"Brown sugar?"

"Yeah."

"Lots of it?"

"She pumps it to him pretty good."

"Then I'd load them all up on it," the doctor recommended. "And, of course, you'll want to replace all the food you've been giving them, then keep a pretty good watch over the new stuff."

"We'll do that," Farrington said firmly. "We'll sure as hell do that."

From that point on, the barn was guarded night and day. Every Farrington caretaker became a watchman, a guard. Any stranger showing up with no reason to be near the barn was treated with a rudeness totally alien to the Farrington operation of old.

In time, the Farrington stock improved. So did Joe Marsh's. But nearly a third of the season was over by the time things were back to normal, and the Farrington horses were earning their way into the winner's circle.

"What a terrible shame," Vivian Farrington commented to her husband in the aftermath of the disastrous period. "Why in the world would someone do such an awful thing to so many horses?"

"To get an edge," Bob explained. "Thugs always look for an edge when a lot of money's at stake. Remember, they picked on two of the best stables on the grounds. When our horses— and Joe's—go to post, they're generally among the favorites. And if you eliminate a couple of favorites from a field, chances are good you can not only pick the winner, but get pretty good odds on him."

"Do you think they were after Willie, too?"

"Especially Willie," Farrington said flatly. "He's the favorite, or near-favorite, every time he races. If you know he can't win, there's a fortune to be made on the other horses in the race.''

"How frightening."

"It's over, thank God. We're putting it back together now, getting on with it. But I think it might be a good idea if we took Willie on the road. Left Chicago for a while. A change of scenery might do him good, get some wins on his card.''

Rambling Willie, tranquilizing drugs and all, had been racing well, but had only two victories to his credit when Farrington put him on a van for Scioto Downs, the handsome, futuristic-looking harness plant on the south side of Columbus, Ohio, in mid May. Herman Brickel, the Scioto racing secretary, had invited Willie to perform there, and it was rather like going home for Bob Farrington, who had learned the racing game in Ohio—much of it at Hilliards Raceway, the crude forerunner to Scioto Downs.

Willie made his first Scioto start on May 17, winning easily in 2:00 2/5. A week later he scored in 1:59 3/5, then came back to win in the mud in 2:04 2/5. He was sporting a four-race win skein when he lined up behind the gate on June 6, but the price of pacing had gone up sharply in the week's interim. In the field were Boyden Hanover, the three-year-old pacing champion of 1974, and Jilley, one of 1975's best sophomore pacers.

Farrington had been trying to make Willie a more versatile performer, racing him on the lead occasionally, rather than always closing with a rush from far back in the field. He followed the new pattern in the Scioto contest, with Willie showing the way past all the striped poles, but had to weather the tightest of photo finishes to discover that he'd scored by a slender nose over Boyden Hanover and driver Billy Herman. The Scioto timer read 1:57 4/5, and Rambling Willie owned a spanking new win record.

Willie left the Ohio track with five wins and a second to show for his six starts. More importantly, his trainer was convinced that the Scioto interlude had made a far better racehorse of him. Willie could now race on the front end as well as close fast, he was a "braver" horse, full of confidence, and he had learned the winning habit. Those valuable lessons began to pay immediate dividends when he arrived back in Chicago, this time at Sportsman's Park.

Farrington's five-year-old, confounding his old fans by setting the pace instead of lollygagging back in the pack, lost a length decision to Mirror Image in his homecoming race, then rolled to five awesome decisions in a row, numbering among his victims some of the best pacers of the day—Rin Tim Tim, Smashing Don, Boyden Hanover, Title Holder, Keystone Smartie and Sir Dalrae.

In his July 18 triumph, he left fast, forged to the front past the quarter pole, then paced away from his four rivals to wind up with a four-length bulge in 1:56 1/5. He had done it so easily that Bob Farrington was unaware that his horse had set a world record for aged gelding pacers over a five-eighths mile racetrack until the track announcer reported it to the crowd.

"Champagne tonight?" he asked Paul Seibert during the general melee in the winner's circle following the record performance.

"Buckets of it," Seibert shouted happily.

Farrington beamed as he walked Willie out of the charmed circle, acknowledging the congratulations of fans along the fence. Since the new win skein had started, Bob had made it a habit to walk Willie—rather than drive him—back to the paddock. Farrington readily admitted that vanity had a little to do with the practice, but he had come to believe that he had a horse that was something beyond the ordinary. Why not add a little color to the show? Besides, the crowd seemed to eat it up.

By August 2, with 1:57 and 1:57 2/5 victories under his harness after the record mile, Willie had raced himself out of competition in the Chicago area. He'd been the heavy favorite in all five of his wins, going off at odds of thirty cents on the dollar in the last, and Chicago racing secretaries simply could not scare up rivals of sufficient quality to save him from being bet off the board. In less than a month of racing at Sportsman's Park, he had netted his owners $65,000 in purses. And worn out his welcome.

It was time to hit the road again, which was no problem. Willie was now a star, capable of drawing fans into racing plants, and several tracks were clamoring for his services. Farrington accepted several of the invitations and called for a van. For the first time in years, he—Bob Farrington—would be traveling extensively. Almost like being on the Grand Circuit, he mused, thinking of how he had knocked the idea when

Lloyd Arnold was deciding to invade the Roarin' Grand.

The Willie road show checked into Wolverine Raceway near Detroit on August 9 and quickly disappointed a crowd of 12,913 by getting trapped in traffic, then interfered with twice within seconds, to finish in a dead-heat for third. The interfering horse, Grover C, was placed back in fifth for his violation, but that was little consolation to the Willie supporters.

The Willie caravan headed north to Greenwood Raceway in Toronto, where the $92,300 Canadian Pacing Derby was there for the taking. But Farrington was disappointed when a large entry caused the stakes contest to be split into a pair of $46,150 divisions. And he was flabbergasted when a threat against Willie was phoned to the racetrack.

"Rambling Willie will not win tonight, because we're going to get to him before the race," some mystery voice told the track's switchboard operator.

The Farringtons and Paul Seibert, rocked earlier by the drugging trauma in Chicago, were badly shaken. They immediately hired an around-the-clock guard for their horse, with the young man to remain the rest of the season. The track veterinarian checked Willie in every possible way and pronounced him fit to race, if his trainer and owners were agreeable. Warily, they were.

Willie was oblivious to the furor swirling about him. Farrington sent him quickly to the front, put down late challenges by Mirror Image and Derby's Gent, and won by a length in 1:58 4/5.

Then, relieved to be moving on, the Willie team headed for the Big Apple.

When Rambling Willie arrived at Roosevelt Raceway, Long Island, for the first time, Farrington asked that he be housed in the John Miritello stable. Miritello, who had been a policeman before plunging into harness racing, had been a Farrington aide from 1964 to 1969. But their relationship was much more than boss-employee; they were close friends then, close friends now. When Bob was injured in the Sportsman's Park accident that altered his career, Miritello not only flew in from New York City to visit, but brought his daughter, a budding nurse, as well. The youngster had cared for Farrington throughout his hospital stay.

Miritello was one of dozens of horsemen that Farrington, with no fanfare whatsoever, had helped financially, career-wise, or both, changing the course of some of their lives in the process. Miritello worshiped him and might have remained a Farrington lieutenant forever had he been able to get along with the gruff and volatile Louie Farrington. As it was, he had left Bob and gone out on his own, doing reasonably well in the New York metropolitan area.

"So this is the famous Rambling Willie," Miritello commented as the pacer arrived at his barn.

"That's him," Farrington confirmed.

"I'll tell ya, Red Man, he don't *look* all that much."

"He gets around a racetrack pretty handy."

"He must," Miritello laughed, "to get you back out on the road."

But Willie had problems on the tight turns of Roosevelt's smaller half-mile track, winding up third behind Mirror Image and Bret's Triumph in the Raceway's $50,000 Old Country Pace. "It was not one of my better drives," Farrington confessed to Miritello after the match.

Down at Brandywine Raceway near Wilmington, Delaware, a week later, Bob was treated like a hero as he returned to the Delaware Valley for the first time in years. Sportswriters recalled that he was a former Brandywine driving champion, that he used to drive a dozen or more times a day as he dashed back and forth between the afternoon races at Freehold Raceway and the evening card at Brandywine, and that he had once won all six of the races he was in at Freehold.

The writers were kind to his new pacing champion, too, and Willie obliged with an almost casual victory in 1:57 2/5 over Mirror Image and the great four-year-old pacing mare of the day, Handle With Care. A week later it was back to the tough turns of the compact Roosevelt Raceway oval, where he could do no better than second. But it was the last race he would lose in the month of September, 1975.

Willie won a pair of free-for-all paces at Northfield Park near Cleveland, scored by four lengths in 2:00 1/5 at The Meadows near Pittsburgh, then turned up at Maywood Park back in Chicago, where he won easily over Mirror Image and company in 1:59 1/5.

Unaccountably, he then went two uninspired trips in a row, losing to Mirror Image and Rin Tim Tim at Maywood, and finishing a dismal seventh at Windsor Raceway, Windsor, Canada.

At Maywood, he was the top-heavy favorite, racing at odds of forty cents to the dollar, but fell victim to Maywood's half-mile track and racing heroics by Mirror Image. Whereas Farrington had been able to send him directly into the lead the week before, he was unable to make the top this time around—that honor went to the Buddy Gilmour-handled Mirror Image—and had to spend the balance of the contest parked out. Willie was a weary pacer when the grueling mile finally ended.

The rocky, energy-sapping journey at Maywood may have led to his downfall at Windsor. Farrington now seemed determined to race him at the front of the pack, but sweet-pacing Handle With Care kept him from that goal until the half, reached in a terribly fast 58 4/5 seconds. Normally, his driver would have given him a short rest in the next quarter, but the Dick Williams-driven Young Quinn would not permit it. Young Quinn sailed right on by and kept going, crossing the finish in a track record-equaling 1:56 3/5. A tired Rambling Willie backed through the pack in the final panel, managing to beat only two horses in the field of nine.

Willie had whipped Young Quinn with ease in September, but Bob Farrington could see that Quinn was a much improved pacer, only now beginning to live up to the press clippings that had accompanied him on his immigration to the United States from New Zealand. Quinn had been touted as "the finest horse to come from Down Under since Cardigan Bay," and Farrington was well aware that Cardigan Bay had been the first pacing horse in the world to earn a million dollars.

It was now mid-October, with racing opportunities for free-for-all pacers dwindling as major racetracks closed their doors for the winter. The logical spot to invade with Willie was Hollywood Park, the giant, handsome racing plant near Los Angeles, but pacing stars like Young Quinn, Handle With Care and Peter Lobell would be there for sure. And Willie, even his biased trainer and owners had to admit, hadn't been that impressive in his last couple of efforts.

The possible expedition to the West was discussed at several pow-wows, until Bob Farrington, the former non-traveler, suggested almost jauntily, "What the heck, let's try it. We haven't been to California lately, and, who knows, Willie might return to form."

"Yeah, and Willie might enjoy a big mile track for a change," Paul Seibert chimed in.

"Good point," said Farrington.

It was a new experience for Rambling Willie, this Hollywood Park. Sticking his head out the stall, seeing palm trees scattered all about, looking up to see two or three airliners passing overhead every minute, bound for Los Angeles International Airport only a few minutes away. Balmy breezes and warm sunshine in the daytime, brisk temperatures at night, perfect for sleeping. A whole new world. A good world.

On October 24 he went postward in a $15,000 race, a tune-up for the $50,000 Western Pace six nights later and the $100,000 American Pacing Classic a week after the Western. Farrington altered his driving style in the tune-up, reverting back to the catch-them-in-the-stretch practice, and it worked. Willie was sixth at the top of the stretch, four lengths behind the leader, but came barreling home in something like 27 seconds to nip Handle With Care and Peter Lobell. The 1:56 1/5 timing equaled both his personal win record and his world mark for aged pacing geldings over a five-eighths mile track. Over the mile track at Hollywood Park, the clocking was also a world record.

Only one other pacing gelding, Armbro Ontario, had ever gone as fast over a big oval. He had set his record the year before as a three-year-old. Willie's reign as the co-record holder was to be much shorter.

Both marks were erased before the week was up, becoming the property of Young Quinn in the $50,000 Western. The New Zealand import, fifth to Willie six nights earlier, beat the Farrington star at his own game. Quinn streaked the last quarter in 27 2/5, passing Willie in the stretch, to win in 1:56. Peter Lobell rubbed salt in the wound by edging Willie for second.

That left the $100,000 Classic as the final major race of the year, with the eight best aged pacers still active in the country entered. Familiar foes Young Quinn, Peter Lobell, Rin Tim Tim, Handle With Care and Mirror Image were present and accounted for, as was Tarport Hap, another tough tomboy mare who had spent a good share of the season racing against the "boys," who are supposed to be faster. It was the first time that several of them—including Rambling Willie—had been called on to race at the mile and an eighth distance.

Handle With Care, Young Quinn and Peter Lobell all took turns at setting the pace before Willie made his move, easing into the lead on the final turn and looking very much like the winner halfway down the stretch. But, then, Young Quinn, driven by the ultra-clever Joe O'Brien, found new life in the drive and ambled up alongside Willie. The timer flashed 2:12 3/5 for the extra-distance contest, and a throng of 17,000 held its collective breath as it awaited the results of the photo finish camera.

The finish was so close that Vivian Farrington urged the owners of Quinn to head for the winner's circle for the trophy ritual. But Quinn's owners were so positive that Willie had won that they convinced Vivian to prance into the circle. She was slipping through the gate when the winner's number went up. It belonged to Young Quinn.

Willie's long and tumultuous season, a grueling nine-month stretch that had included a sustained period of drugging, a threat to his safety, more than ten thousand miles of travel, and competition against the very best pacers of the day, was over.

His thirty-seven races had produced nineteen wins, eight seconds and eight thirds, along with a new personal (and world) record of 1:56 1/5. Astoundingly, he had failed to earn a check in only one of his starts, and his total earnings for 1975 stood at a thumping $264,405.

"You're going to have to find yourself a tax shelter, Paul," a blissful Bob Farrington advised Paul Seibert in late December.

"A little late for that," Seibert answered seriously, "with the end of 1975 only a few days away."

"Who's talking about 1975? I mean for next year."

"Next year? You can't be serious. Willie's going to be six years old in '76. He can't earn that kind of money again."

"I could be wrong, dead wrong, but I think he can," Bob said thoughtfully. "Of course, he's got to stay sound to do it."

Chapter 12

Short of a broken leg or neck, harness horsemen fear a bowed tendon more than any of the thousand and one other injuries that can befall a horse. When a horse "bows," the fibers making up the tendon running from knee to ankle in a front leg are stretched and torn, leaving the calf swollen, mushy, hot and terribly painful. A bowed tendon has probably forced more horses into retirement than any other ailment. And those that have survived have rarely, if ever, returned to the racing form they once owned.

Rambling Willie bowed his right tendon on March 24, 1976, bringing Bob Farrington's racing world crashing down upon him.

Willie had raced in a qualifying contest that morning, using the non-purse event as a final tightener for the racing season about to start. Farrington had noticed that he seemed a trifle lame moments after the race, but thought little of it. Willie, at six years, was now an "old man" in the racing game, and old men were known to possess a few aches and pains when they continued to mix it with younger foes in professional athletics.

The injury was discovered when groom Mike Martin began to unwind the racing bandage from the leg. "Bob!" Martin screamed, bringing Farrington into Willie's stall on the dead run.

"My God," Farrington moaned when he spotted the tendon.

"Is it bad?" the caretaker demanded, his voice quivering.

"Bad? Yeah, I'd say it's bad, Mike. I'd say there's a good

chance he's finished,'' the trainer answered softly.

Tears rushed to Mike Martin's eyes, while the familiar curtain of stoicism descended upon Farrington's face. Farrington was a master at patching up ailing horses, had made a career out of it. But he had never had much luck with horses afflicted with bowed tendons. Nor had his father, Louie Farrington, who had performed minor miracles with scores of problem horses at the family's recuperation center at Richwood, Ohio.

''Put the hose on the leg while I hunt up a vet,'' Farrington instructed the young groom before hustling off to find medical assistance.

Bob was sitting on Willie's tack trunk, head bowed, eyes fastened to the ground, when Vivian arrived at the barn.

''Willie's hurt,'' she said matter-of-factly.

Farrington had long since given up any attempt to understand his wife's ability to accurately perceive a situation without benefit of information of any kind. ''Hurt bad,'' he told her flatly. ''He's bowed a tendon.''

Vivian stared at her husband for a long moment. ''It could be worse,'' she said finally.

''I don't see how,'' Bob growled. He loved his wife dearly, but her placid nature, the calmness with which she could receive and accept disaster of any magnitude, was sometimes aggravating.

''With prayer and Dad's salve . . .'' Vivian suggested gently.

In spite of himself, Bob smiled. Then he began to feel a bit better, a bit brighter. Bless her, Vivian always had that effect on him. Nothing was ever hopeless, nothing was ever impossible. With prayer and Dad's salve . . .

''We'll give it a try, Viv,'' he sighed, hopping off the trunk. ''Damned if we won't give it a try.''

''It'll turn out all right,'' she said.

Few agreed with her. By the time Paul Seibert heard news of the ruptured tendon and made tracks for Chicago, Willie was the talk of the Washington Park backstretch. Most of the backstretch dwellers had already written him off. Rambling Willie is through, they were saying, their voices soft and sad, as though some much admired contemporary had died.

Seibert, arriving at Washington Park, couldn't find Farrington, so he wandered from barn to barn, badgering other horsemen. "What's the prognosis in a case like this? What're his chances of coming back?" he probed.

Most hedged. A few offered false optimism. But Jim Dolbee, one of the younger, more outspoken trainers, was gentle, yet frank. "Paul," he said, "don't get your hopes up. The odds are against him racing again. And even if he does, he might only be a shadow of what he was."

Seibert gulped, but nodded his thanks.

"But the nicest part of what I told you," Dolbee added, "is that I could be dead wrong. And I hope to hell I am."

Bob Farrington, once found, offered a mixed potion of guarded hope and plain pessimism. The two veterinarians treating Willie offered the same message, but with less hope. Vivian Farrington, unruffled, unshaken, was adamant that Willie would bounce back, would pick up his racing career as though the injury had never happened.

"Are we going to use the reverend's salve on him?" Paul inquired, flashing his first grin since learning of Willie's misfortune.

The reverend's salve was something to joke about, but hardly a joke. Vivian's father, the Reverend C. L. Harris, manufactured by hand—and sold—a medicine he called "The Balm of Gilead," a combination of two hoary recipes he had collected in his long career as a small town pastor in Central Ohio. The ingredients were mutton tallow, beeswax, resin, oil of sassafras, linseed oil, oil of red cedar, gum of camphor, and something called oil of organim. Blended, they seemed to cure a regular cornucopia of human ailments.

Mr. Harris had received written or verbal testimonials from people who said The Balm of Gilead had defeated fungus, ulcers, ingrown toenails, poison ivy, warts, corns, burns, sores of all kinds, and a wide range of bumps and bruises. Asked once what his salve could heal, Harris had answered promptly, "I don't know what it can't heal."

Its greatest attribute, users claimed, was that it was most effective in relieving pain.

The Harris children—Vivian, her sister and brothers—had used it for years, swearing by its healing properties. The Farringtons, too, once Bob and Vivian had united the families, swore by it and used it regularly. And Paul Seibert's mother had been helped by it after all known drugs had failed to relieve her lameness.

The Balm of Gilead was a staple in the Farrington racing barn, and had been since the day that Bob had deduced that anything that effective against human hurts would likely be beneficial to horses, too. The reverend's salve had been used on most of Farrington's horses over the years, including Rambling Willie.

A multi-pronged attack was launched on Willie's bowed tendon. The veterinarians were treating him with whatever scientific tools they carried in their heads and their black bags. Farrington was using age-old methods passed on to him by his father and other veteran horsemen. The Balm of Gilead was being rubbed into the tendon faithfully. And, it came to light later, Mike Martin was treating him with an exotic concoction recommended by some ancient caretaker he had met.

Vivian Farrington, her faith as strong as ever, was using prayer and tithing to overcome the twisted, torn, ravaged tendon. "I realize the day will come when we'll have to quit with Willie," she told Bob. "But the Lord has made it very clear to me that this isn't the time."

Her husband was ready to believe her. Willie's progress was astounding. In a matter of days, the fever and the pain had both fled from the calf of his leg. Some of the swelling remained—would always be there—but it was concentrated in an area low on the leg, the thickened area firm, almost hard, and cool to the touch. And he seemed sound.

"It's a miracle," Al Bernard pronounced.

"Talk to Vivian about that," Farrington responded happily.

In mid-April, the horse that was supposed to be finished, supposed to be lounging in some pasture, was being harnessed and driven to the training track for his first jogging session since suffering the injury. A pair of grizzled caretakers, veterans of countless years of rubbing horses and living in tackrooms, applauded when they recognized Willie stepping onto the track. There were grins on every face that Farrington and Willie passed on the training oval.

"Way to go, Willie," trainers and grooms offered warmly. "Congratulations, Bob," they said. "Can't keep the old guy down . . . Tough old buzzard, Bob . . . Nice to see you back,

Willie . . . Go get 'em, Willie . . . Couldn't happen to a greater horse, Bob . . . Watch out, Free-For-Allers, Willie's back. . . ."

Bob Farrington, tough, Spartan, unemotional, forever Mr. Cool, had a schoolboy-like fear that he would burst into tears before the session was over. He completed the last lap, then, striving to regain his composure, headed his pacer back to the barn.

"How'd he go?" Bernard asked anxiously.

"Didn't do nothing but jog, but he seems as good as ever," Farrington answered slowly.

"I tell ya, Bob, if we opened that son-of-a-gun up, I guarantee we'd find a heart in him ten times the size of a normal one."

"You get no argument from me, Cat," Bob agreed.

On May 16, fifty-three days after Farrington's pacer had sustained one of racing's most devastating injuries, Washington Park ran an advertisement in a number of Chicago area papers that said, "World Champion Rambling Willie Returns Today!" That afternoon he finished third in a $10,000 Preferred Pace, individually timed in 1:57 2/5. A week later he paced a 1:59 mile to defeat seven of the toughest horses on the grounds.

Rambling Willie had not only returned to the races, but was as fit, fast and feisty as ever. He had defied most of the logic and lore that had accumulated in one hundred and seventy years of harness racing history. And he had scoffed at, bent, circumvented and ignored the rules of modern veterinary science.

Indeed, Willie Boy was back.

The racing scene shifted to Sportsman's Park, and Willie went with it. He was third in a pair of cheap contests, which did not disturb his trainer. Farrington's mind was on the second leg of the U.S. Pacing Championship.

As usual, a heavy entry—thirteen horses—caused the June 12 stakes affair to be split into a pair of $40,000 divisions, with Willie drawing in with the three-year-old superstar of the prior year, Nero. Nero, a son of Meadow Skipper, had recently been syndicated for $3.6 million, the most ever paid for a standardbred, and Farrington thought it would be great fun to beat him with an aging campaigner with pedestrian breeding who was coming off a bowed tendon.

Vivian Farrington had a simpler reason for wanting to defeat Nero. Her father and mother made a habit of stopping in a small Mt. Victory, Ohio, restaurant after church each Sunday. One of the waitresses was a Nero fan who claimed she'd never heard of Rambling Willie. "When your Willie horse beats my Nero, then I'll acknowledge his existence," she was fond of saying.

Willie, a six-to-one underdog, stalked the front-running Keystone Accent for most of the Pacing Championship mile, inheriting the lead when the erratic pacesetter jumped off stride at the head of the stretch. Farrington knew what to expect next—a late charge by Nero—and wound Willie up accordingly. Nero, whipped out and slashed down the lane by driver Joe O'Brien, gave it a gutsy try, but was still short at the end. Willie had his Championship victory in 1:57 1/5, and the Reverend and Mrs. C. L. Harris had their friendly retribution in the Mt. Victory restaurant.

While the waitress was sincere in her devotion to Nero, she was simply having fun with the Harrises when she claimed she hadn't heard of Rambling Willie. By this time, the secret of Vivian Farrington's tithing of Willie's earnings was out, spreading across the nation, beginning to make headlines. The residents of Mt. Victory—all of them—had known of it for months.

Vivian had done her best to keep it a private matter, something strictly between her and God. Parishioners and leaders of the Church of Christ had been close-mouthed about it, too. For a variety of reasons. However, Vivian had let it slip in a conversation with a horseman named, ironically, Jim Curran.

Curran was no relation to the Farringtons' son-in-law, Jim Curran, although the similarity of their names—one was James M., the other James R. Curran—had always led to considerable confusion in racing circles. James M. was still handling all the Farrington horses except Rambling Willie in Chicago; James R. habitually campaigned along the East Coast.

The East Coast's Jim Curran, chatting with Vivian during Willie's race at Brandywine Raceway, Delaware, in 1975 had asked her how she and Bob managed to keep a veteran performer like Willie racing so sharply, so successfully week after week.

"It's easy," Vivian had replied. "I tithe ten percent of his earnings to the Lord, then the Lord keeps him going."

Curran was fascinated, pressing her for details. Vivian willingly supplied them. Curran, as he went about his racing business, couldn't forget the conversation. Months later, in chatting with a U.S. Trotting Association publicity man, he had mentioned the tithing when the subject of Rambling Willie came up.

"What did you say Vivian Farrington does?" the USTA staffer asked, mystified.

"Tithes," Curran repeated. "Donates ten percent of her share of Rambling Willie's earnings to God. To the Church of Christ in West Mansfield, Ohio, to be precise. Her father's the pastor there."

"Incredible!" the publicist muttered. "Great story."

Arriving back at the USTA's headquarters in Columbus, Ohio, the publicity man had immediately contacted Vivian. Grudgingly, almost guiltily, she answered his questions. With even more reluctance, Reverend Harris followed suit. The Trotting Association, forever anxious to cast a warm and favorable light upon the harness sport, released the news to the media. The build-up started slowly, with a newspaper here, a newspaper there using it. Then the wire services—the Associated Press and United Press International—started to pick up on it. The columnists began to call for more information. The magazines became interested. For the rest of his racing career, Willie would be known as "The Horse that Supports a Church."

To keep that church supported, Willie had to earn purses, and that was Farrington's goal as he took him back out on the road. He raced once more at Sportsman's Park, closing from seventh to get within a neck of world champion pacing mare Tarport Hap in 1:57 2/5, then moved on to Roosevelt Raceway on Long Island. At Roosevelt on June 26 he started his charge from ninth position, made up more than seven lengths in the rush to the wire, but could finish no better than third. A week later at Scioto Downs near Columbus he fell a neck short to Pickwick Baron as the Baron, driven by Mel Turcotte, paced the five-eighths mile track in 1:56—a world and track record for aged stallions.

He was back at Sportsman's Park on July 12, nipping

tough rivals Rusty Knight and Young Quinn in 1:59 2/5. Seven nights later, he scored over the same foes in two minutes flat, then got hopelessly parked out over the same track on the night of July 24, finishing a well beaten fourth. The Willie team decided to send him on to the $61,600 Canadian Pacing Derby at Greenwood Raceway, Toronto, on July 31, but wondered if his tight edge had survived the rugged race in Chicago.

The Farringtons, along with Paul Seibert, could well remember Willie's appearance in the 1975 edition of the Derby. Their pacer had won his division easily, but the visit had been marred by a telephone threat against him, robbing the triumph of some of its luster. A bad race in Chicago, tougher competition, and an unfavorable seven-post made it unlikely that he would repeat as a Derby winner.

"Let's hope he races at least fairly well for your parents," Seibert whispered to Vivian.

Reverend and Mrs. Harris were with them in the Greenwood clubhouse, about to see their daughter's famous horse for the first time. Mr. Harris was sitting ramrod straight in his chair, like a Prussian general in mufti, but his lively eyes were darting every which way, taking in the busy scene around him—hostesses seating people, waitresses scurrying from table to table, pretty girls in charming uniforms writing betting tickets.

"Does it bother you to be here, Reverend, knowing that people around you are gambling?" Seibert asked.

"Oh, no," the clergyman answered swiftly. "What people do with their money is their own business. I wouldn't encourage it, mind you, but it doesn't seem to be a great deal different than people playing the stock market. Of course, I don't gamble. Never have, never will . . . ."

"There have been times when I've wished I could say that," Seibert said, laughing.

"Lots of those nights, Paul," Vivian offered. Then she added, "Dad, Mother, look. There's Willie."

Announcer Earl Lennox was introducing the horses for the Derby—Shirley's Beau, Napal Dew, Young Quinn, Mirror Image, Albert's Star, Jambo Dancer, Meadow Blue Chip and Rambling Willie. Willie, wearing one of the new modified sulkies—sleeker, more slender, said to be faster—was passing in front of the clubhouse.

"So that's the horse that's meant so much to my little church," Harris said brightly.

"That's him," Vivian announced proudly. "But, Dad, I really wouldn't count on him for much help tonight . . ." she started to add.

"Oh, I don't know about that," Seibert interrupted. Slowly, almost slyly, he pulled his right hand from the pocket of his sports jacket. In the hand, folded once, was a personal check, which he handed to the reverend.

"What's this?" Harris asked, surprised. "Paul, it's a check for two thousand dollars, made out to the West Mansfield Church of Christ. Now why would you do a thing like that . . .?"

Seibert, bold only a moment before, was suddenly overcome with shyness. "I don't know exactly . . ." he stammered. "I wanted to do it. I guess it's because I've been around your daughter so much that some of her charity's sort of rubbed off on me. Or . . . maybe it's because old Willie seems to make me money faster than I can spend it."

"Well, I pretty much doubt *that*," Reverend Harris said firmly, earning a round of laughter.

But the reverend was wrong, Seibert closer to right.

Five minutes later, Rambling Willie, bad post, tough competition and all, was flashing under the wire, a length and a half ahead of everyone else in the Derby field. The time was 1:57 4/5, the fastest clocking of the year in Canada and only one-fifth of a second off the Greenwood track record.

Half the $30,800 he had picked up in his swift tour belonged to Paul Seibert.

Co-owners Paul Seibert and Viv Farrington join Bob in collecting a pair of Rambling Willie's annual awards.

Willie bought the church's new sign, but the Farringtons got the credit.

Below, a dejected Bob Farrington contemplates Rambling Willie's future after the horse suffered his first bowed tendon.

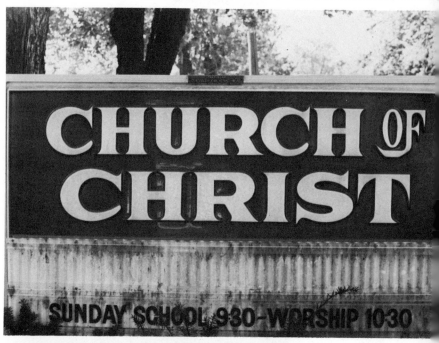

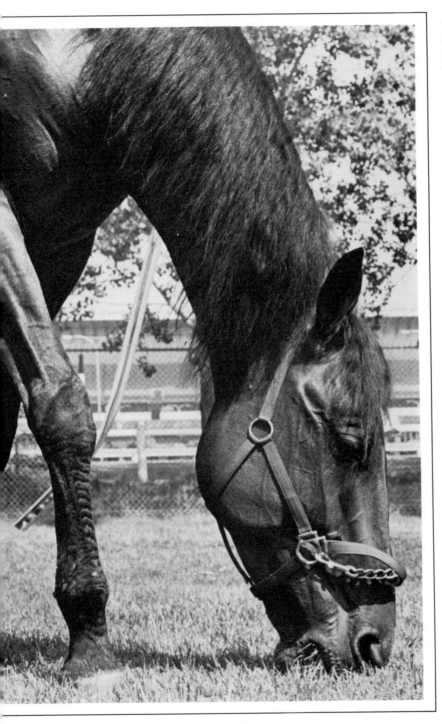

The ravages to Willie's right leg are obvious, although he seems oblivious. *Michael Burns photo.*

Bob Farrington and Jim Curran laugh it up during a break in the morning training routine.

Right, the West Mansfield Church of Christ — the church that Rambling Willie redecorated.

Below, football great Joe Namath and Sonny Werblin (far right) were among the well wishers after Rambling Willie won the feature race on the night the mighty Meadowlands opened.

Far Right, Farrington and his wife are congratulated by Phil Langley of Sportman's Park in a small winner's circle ceremony after the teamster's 3000th career win. (The horse is not Willie.)

The magnificent mare Handle
With Care (7) was not tough
enough to catch Rambling
Willie in the $50,000 Good
Time Pace at Yonkers
Raceway. *Michael Cipriani
photo.*

Below, Rambling Willie
coasts home an easy winner
at Maywood Park.

Chapter 13

N*orthbound* traffic on the New Jersey Turnpike was extremely heavy, culminating in a wretched, temper-provoking snarl at Exit 16W. The aged tunnels—Lincoln and Holland—linking Manhattan, Brooklyn, Queens and Long Island with New Jersey were reeking with exhaust, clogged with horn-honking cars. The George Washington Bridge was bumper to bumper. Closer in, Routes 3, 17 and 21 were jammed. So were Erie and Union Avenues, along with Hackensack Street.

A new racetrack—The Meadowlands—was opening in East Rutherford, New Jersey, and not even the most optimistic of its shakers, movers and builders had anticipated a horde like the one descending upon the racing palace from every direction. They called it *The House that Sonny Built*, "Sonny" being David Werblin, the man who had bought the floundering New York football Titans, turned them into the Jets, hired Joe Namath as quarterback, and changed the face of professional football. Then Sonny had accepted an even greater challenge—spearheading the construction of the $302 million New Jersey Sports Complex, with The Meadowlands track as the first shimmering jewel in the glittering, grandiose scheme.

It was the evening of September 1, 1976, and by 7:15, every seat in the new temple had a rump in it. The 28,000 racing programs printed for opening night were gone by 7:30. And still the fans poured in, cursing the highway crush they had survived to get there, but marveling at the titanic tossed salad of concrete, steel, glass, and bright, multicolored lights served up by the new edifice.

For safety's sake, State Police officers closed the gates after 42,133 souls had thundered through, but it did no good. Another 10,000 or so, frustrated by the wars on the Turnpike and in the tunnels, seething because they'd had to park in no man's land, stormed the gates, brushed the officers aside, and scurried in without paying.

The total crowd threatened, if not exceeded, harness racing's grandest ever, the 54,861 collected by Roosevelt Raceway to witness its International Trot in 1960.

The vast majority had shown up to celebrate, to participate in, a "Happening"—another Woodstock, an Indianapolis 500, a Kentucky Derby, the opening of a new shopping center. But some of the folks pushing and shoving to establish a small, personal command post were there for their first, second, third or fourth glimpse of the new idol of the metropolitan New York fans, ageless Rambling Willie.

Willie, racing as a five-year-old in 1975, had dazzled racing buffs everywhere but in New York. He had been a disappointment in both his contests at Roosevelt Raceway, finishing third and second. But that was 1975.

After winning the 1976 Canadian Pacing Derby at Toronto, Farrington had shipped him down to Yonkers Raceway, lodging him again in the New York-based barn of John Miritello. Then he had turned him loose over the half-mile Yonkers oval, ignoring the fact that its short stretch was bound to be a disadvantage to a late-charging pacer like Willie.

A lukewarm betting favorite, he made his Yonkers debut on August 7, shooting out of the pack in the final turn to edge Shirley's Beau and Napal Dew in 1:58 3/5. His next invitation was to an event called the Kilmore Trotting Club Trophy Pace, a mile and a quarter contest named for an Australian racing organization. Willie had never competed at a mile and a quarter before, but he seemed perfectly contented to contribute a touch of overtime, pacing to victory in 2:29 2/5 and lowering the world record for pacing geldings of any age at the extra distance. Bob Farrington was a happy horseman as he walked the record-holder back to the paddock.

It was the best of times for both Rambling Willie and his trainer. While Willie was resting between engagements at Yonkers, Farrington was making forays back into the Chicago area, trying to earn himself another niche in harness racing history.

Bob was generally oblivious to such things, but Phil Langley, the tall, bespectacled racing secretary at Sportsman's Park, had noticed at the start of the 1976 season that Farrington was only thirteen victories away from the three thousand mark. Only seven American drivers before him had reached that milestone, and Langley was determined that Bob would become the eighth. And that it would happen at Sportsman's Park.

"I don't have much interest in that kind of thing," Farrington protested.

"Well, your friends and fans do," Langley insisted, lecturing him like he was a freshman back in Rushsylvania High School. "You're going to drive enough to hit three thousand by mid-season, and we're going to time it so that it happens at Sportsman's, where you've won so many championships and where the fans appreciate you the most."

"You're the boss," Farrington capitulated.

Rambling Willie had contributed seven wins to the Red Man's collection. In addition, Farrington had won four other races in recent weeks, driving an occasional horse here and there to keep the determined Langley off his back. When Willie scooted under the Yonkers' wire to snap the world mark, he was a single win short of three thousand. And Langley was on the phone.

"I'm coming," Farrington said resignedly.

It was the tenth and last race on the Sportsman's program on the evening of August 17, when the ex-bricklayer from Richwood, Ohio, now in his twenty-first season at the races, reached his—and Phil Langley's—goal. But the record-setting win was anti-climactic at best. The Tuesday night crowd, sparse to begin with, was down to dregs, folks who were hoping to get even in the tenth race trifecta, when Farrington went to post with Captain Conte in a $12,000 claiming contest. Their applause was more than polite, but the event was hardly what Langley had envisioned as Bob brought the veteran pacer home a length winner.

Farrington treated the affair lightly, like an obligation he had successfully fulfilled. His family and friends were determined to make an occasion out of it, however. John Miritello had flown in from New York on the chance that his ex-boss and revered friend would reach the milestone that night. Mrs.

Harold Brown, the wife of another former Farrington aide, had driven up from Springfield, Illinois. Joe and Adele Vollaro, two of the Farringtons' closest friends, were there, too, as the group headed for the Contessa Del Mar, a lively restaurant in nearby Alsip, Illinois. The party, which did not get under way until 1:00 a.m., was still going strong at breakfast time.

It was like Christmas morning for the newest member of harness racing's Three Thousand Win Club. Miritello conferred a diamond bracelet on Farrington, wife Vivian gave him a diamond horseshoe pendant, and Mr. and Mrs. Jay Stone, co-owners of the horse that had provided Bob with his milestone triumph, presented him with a handsome cigarette lighter. All of the glittering pieces had "3,000" inscribed on them.

Then it was time to head back to Yonkers. Rambling Willie had two more very tough races in his immediate future there.

The first was the $75,000 Hudson Valley Pace, a mile and a half endurance test that saw Handle With Care, the Bill Haughton-driven mare, go the race of her lifetime, pushing into the lead at the first quarter pole and never relinquishing it. Several of her adversaries, all but one of them rugged males, took shots at her during the three trips around the half-mile oval, but without success. Rambling Willie's late splurge was the grittiest of them all, yet he could not close the gap on the flying female, either. Handle With Care traveled the final four furlongs in 58 2/5, leaving Willie two lengths back in second and halting his current win streak at three. The mare's 3:01 4/5 timing eclipsed the 3:02 3/5 world mark for the distance, set seven years earlier by a powerhouse pacer called Overtrick.

It figured that Handle With Care would be the bettors' choice in the next meeting between the two a week later in a $50,000 free-for-all. Not so, however. The Yonkers plungers still preferred Willie, sent him off at even money, and were rewarded with one of the finest outings of his career. The son of Rambling Fury seemed trapped back in the pack until Farrington took him off the rail and began to edge closer to the leaders. Straightening out for home, it looked like a replay of the last race, with Handle With Care in the lead and Willie scrambling to overtake her. But this time he swept past the female champ with plenty of time to spare, going on to win the mile test in 1:57 1/5. Only a glance at the record book was necessary to confirm that he was now history's fastest aged gelding over a half-mile track.

Three Yonkers victories, two of them in record time, were on his card as Joe De Frank, racing secretary of the new Meadowlands, went about inviting North America's finest free-for-all pacers to the track's inaugural feature race. Farrington was among the first to hear from the persuasive De Frank.

Ironically, The Meadowlands was opening on the same evening that Brandywine Raceway in Wilmington had scheduled its annual General Mad Anthony for aged pacing stars. Farrington hated to miss the Mad Anthony—he'd won it in 1975 with Willie—yet he chose to accept The Meadowlands' invitation. When the trainers of most of the big pacers arrived at the same decision—the lure of being part of opening night at the new track was too great—the Brandywine event was postponed. It was one of the early indications of the immense impact the innovative, state-run Meadowlands would have on the sport of harness racing.

Vivian Farrington and Paul Seibert, as owners of one of the chosen performers in the inaugural feature, were treated with great deference by the management of the sport's new flagship track. They thoroughly enjoyed themselves in the splendor of the vast clubhouse restaurant, ogling famous personalities like New Jersey Governor Brendan Byrne, Joe Namath and Telly Savalas as they walked by, and thanking their lucky stars they were not in the crush of humanity trying to reach betting windows, concession stands, drinking fountains and bathrooms in the grandstand. It was a night to remember even if Willie failed to win, which was quite likely.

The Meadowlands, planning to offer thoroughbred racing half the year, had constructed a mile-around track. The bigger the track, the faster it is, so it figured that a profusion of swift miles would be recorded over it as time went by. The speedy miles were not expected in the beginning, however, because problems had cropped up with the racing surface. It was "cupping out," sticking to horses' shoes, coming up in small clods, leaving hundreds of shallow holes. As late as the afternoon of the opening program, workmen were laboring frenziedly to correct its ills.

The track, of course, would be the same for all ten horses in the $50,000 Premier Pace, Willie's event. But Willie was racing with only five days rest, and was leaving from the eight-post.

Seibert, the eternal bettor, noticed with some satisfaction, however, that several of Willie's rivals were still wearing the old conventional sulky. Willie, on the other hand, was tugging the new modified bike. Conservative horsemen were still fighting the new sulky; Farrington had put it on Willie as soon as one had become available. Seibert headed for the mutuel windows with a secret smile on his face.

Willie was shunted back to ninth in the early going and remained there until the leaders reached the half-pole in a fearsome 57 1/5. There was no gaining on anyone with the field going that fast, so Farrington played a waiting game. On the backside of the track he began to tap Willie, creeping gradually up on the outside of other horses. Willie was parked out, going a longer route than the pacers inside him, but he felt fresh and strong to Farrington's hands.

As the fancy field swooshed past the three-quarter pole in 1:25 3/5, Farrington's pacer was third and still moving. Halfway down the stretch Bob could hear the familiar "Will-eeee! Will-eeee!" chant booming from the jam-packed grandstand, and he went to the whip. Suddenly he was on top, leading the field in the first feature race offered by the mighty Meadowlands. Farrington knew that Nero was coming hard, so he continued to bounce the whip off Willie's saddlepad. He held his breath as the finish came and went with Nero getting no closer than a length and a half.

Racing secretary Joe De Frank had put a great deal of effort into building a formidable racing program for opening night. Earlier races, despite problems with the racing surface, had gone in impressive times—2:02 1/5, 2:01 1/5, 2:00 1/5, 1:59 4/5 and 1:57 2/5. The knowledgeable crowd had been duly impressed. Now, as Willie's time appeared on the big board, it let loose with a howitzer-like roar.

Caretaker Mike Martin read 1:55 3/5 on the timer and leaped into the air, his right arm striking mighty blows through the night air. Mike was now the groom on the fastest pacing gelding of any age in harness racing history.

Vivian and Seibert had to struggle hard to reach the winner's circle. The crowd was dense, and people who recognized them as the owners of Willie delayed their progress with handshakes and words of congratulations. The girl running the elevator down to the ground level was new—so was the elevator—and left them off on the wrong floor. And, once they reached the circle, they were too excited to fathom the mechanism opening the gate, so they crawled over the fence. Meanwhile, Bob was driving Willie in lazy circles, waiting for them. He knew the owners would never forgive him if he headed for the paddock before they had a chance to pose for a picture with their world champion.

Everyone was laughing—Vivian Farrington, disheveled for one of the few times in her life; Seibert, limping a little from his bout with the fence; Farrington, now climbing out of the sulky; the trophy presenters, who included actor Savalas; and thousands of fans, who had thrilled to Willie's victory and were now enjoying the bit of after-the-race slapstick.

It was a euphoric moment to savor, but the euphoria ended abruptly the very next morning.

Bob and Vivian had flown back to Ohio that night, promising Seibert a fitting celebration the next time they got together. Farrington had to be back in the Buckeye State to race a pair of colts on the fair circuit.

Seibert remained overnight in a motel outside The Meadowlands, turning up in the stable area early Thursday morning. Mike Martin, with red-rimmed eyes and a long, sad face, was waiting for him.

"Bad, bad news, Paul," the young groom announced anxiously.

"What's wrong?"

"Willie's bowed again. Same leg, but worse than last time."

"How's it possible?" Seibert demanded. "My God, he won in 1:55 and a piece last night."

"I don't know," Martin said miserably. "That soft track maybe . . . I don't know. All I know is, he's in terrible shape."

Seibert had to agree. The calf of Willie's right leg was almost grotesque with swelling. Paul had seen the bow at its worst in February, but the new injury seemed even more severe. He reached down and touched the swelling, feeling the heat, noticing the horse flinch and shift his weight.

"We'd better call Bob right away," he told the caretaker.

"We sure as hell better," Martin agreed emphatically.

"This horse is scheduled to fly out to California this afternoon."

"I know that," Willie's co-owner said bitterly.

Seibert phoned the brick farmhouse in Richwood, Ohio, at least a dozen times over the next two hours, raising no one. Bob and Vivian were off to some small Ohio fair, he knew, but he was damned if he could remember which one. And it was doubtful that relatives and friends would have known, either, had he been able to reach them. For the thirteenth or fourteenth time, he slammed the phone into its cradle and headed back to Willie's stall.

"What do we do now?" Martin pressed, near panic. "California or no? You got to decide soon, 'cause the van's on the way to take him to the airport."

Paul Seibert detested his predicament. A decision like that was totally alien to him; Bob Farrington always fielded them. But Bob couldn't be reached. Paul took a deep breath and said, "California. That was the game plan and we'd better stick with it, bowed tendon or not."

"Right," said Martin, who was to accompany the pacer out to Hollywood Park.

Seibert flew back to Cincinnati, phoning the Farringtons from the airport, and then from his home. They did not answer. Early the next morning—Friday—he phoned again, reaching Bob.

"I know all about it, Paul. I've been talking to Bobby Gordon," Farrington said.

Gordon was a thirty-five-year-old horseman from York Center, Ohio, who was making his home at Garden Grove, California, and racing at Hollywood Park. A friend of the Farringtons, he was John Miritello's counterpart on the West Coast—providing a temporary home for Farrington horses like Rambling Willie.

"What's Bobby say?" Seibert asked anxiously.

"That Willie got in about six last night California time. That he's in terrible shape, with both the sheath and the tendons apparently ruptured. That the leg may be beyond repair."

Seibert groaned.

"Doctor Buckley's flying out from Cleveland to check him," Farrington explained. "But, Paul," he added soberly, "I've got to warn you, from what I've heard, I'd have to think he's gone his last mile."

"I suppose . . ." Seibert said, his voice cracking, "it had to end sometime."

"Yeah, it did. But remember, Willie made us more than $600,000, set a bunch of records, did everything you can ask a horse to do. I really believe it's a time to be grateful, rather than sad." The trainer's tone was flat, soft, without emotion, like he had come to grips with some great trauma, survived it, and now was intent upon getting on with life.

"You're right, of course, Bob," Seibert said, suddenly realizing that Farrington was losing a great deal more than Willie's owners were. Without Willie, Bob's comeback, his second coming, his second journey to center stage, was over. There would be no more Rambling Willies in his future. Probably in anybody's future.

"Paul, get up and see us when you can," the trainer urged.

"This weekend," the owner promised, then asked, "By the way, how's Vivian taking it?"

"I don't think it's sunk in yet. At least, she doesn't seem very broken up. But, then, you know Viv; probably figures she's going to cure old Willie with a prayer."

"Yeah," Seibert said. "Yeah."

Vivian Farrington was not broken up. Reserved, quiet, introspective, yes; but not broken up, not depressed. While Bob was in the house, she puttered softly about, straightening this, cooking that. When he was outside, fooling with the horses stabled at the farm, or keeping his own counsel, she was reading her Bible, hunting for an answer, an antidote for the new disaster. And she never—not once—doubted that she would find it.

It came early Sunday afternoon, while Bob Farrington was out in the barn, while Paul Seibert was driving up from Cincinnati.

She found it in the *Living Bible*, the smaller, paraphrased version of the master work, a volume she consulted daily and without fail. The passage she sought was in Mark 11:24 and 25. Jesus was addressing the disciples. *"Listen to me! You can pray for anything, and if you believe, you have it; it's yours! But when you are praying, first forgive anyone you are holding a grudge against, so that your Father in heaven will forgive you your sins too."* TLB

Vivian Farrington, with a heart filled with precisely the

kind of faith that Jesus had prescribed, bowed her head and fell softly to her knees. Only the whir of an electric clock disturbed the silence as she took Jesus at His word, erasing from her mind any and all malice she had ever held for anyone, then humbly asking God for help once again in curing a horse that now meant so very much to so very many.

No finger touched her, no voice spoke to her, no bright light blinded her. But at some point in her prayer, in her long and intense meditation, a *feeling* descended upon her, a soft and warm and comfortable, yet vibrant, sensation that made her *know*, that left no doubt, that her entreaty had been answered.

It was, she told listeners later, often bringing tears to their eyes, the most moving, the most *religious* moment of her life.

When she climbed to her feet, she was convinced, she *knew*, that Rambling Willie was sound, that Bob Gordon would call to confirm it, and that Willie would not only race six nights later, but win that race.

She did not tell her husband of her revelation, not even after Bob Gordon had called to report, with genuine awe, that Rambling Willie, somehow, was sound. That seemingly overnight he had shaken off the injury of all injuries, a bowed tendon. That the swelling was gone, the fever gone, the pain gone. That Willie was bouncing around in his stall like a colt, growing ornery from inactivity.

She told Bob later. She told Paul Seibert almost immediately, as he walked from his car to the Farringtons' front door, head drooping, still shaken by the end of Willie's career, still fearing that Bob would upbraid him for sending the horse to California in such a state.

"Willie's all right," she shouted gaily as Seibert stopped in his tracks and stared at her, recalling later that he felt Vivian had lost her sanity over their joint tragedy.

"Paul, the answer was in the Bible . . ." she said, grabbing his arm, marching him into the family room, and forcing him to read the passages from Mark.

Later, alone with Bob, Paul asked if Bob Gordon, indeed, had said Willie was healed.

"He sure as hell did," Farrington answered. "Said the horse was dead lame in the morning, but sound a few hours later. Said he'd never seen anything like it in his life."

"How do you figure it?" Seibert, forever the devil's advocate, probed.

"I'm not sure. Maybe some great work by Doctor Buckley. Or maybe the old horse wasn't nearly as bad off as you guys figured . . . ."

"Oh, no," Seibert protested. "I saw him and you got to believe he was bad, real bad."

"Must have been Buckley, then," Farrington said flatly.

"Maybe," Seibert said doubtfully.

Six days later, the Farringtons and Paul Seibert flew to Los Angeles, where Rambling Willie was entered in the $50,000 final leg of the U.S. Pacing Championship. Farrington checked his leg, found it healed, but still wondered whether he should start him.

"I'll tell you," he told Paul in the Hollywood Park paddock, "I'll race him if the rains hold off and the track stays dry. But if it comes down in buckets like they're forecasting, I'd rather not take a chance with him. I can scratch him right up to the moment he goes to post, and I will."

Seibert worried and fidgeted throughout dinner as huge, low hung, vicious-looking clouds rolled over the Hollywood racing plant.

"Why so nervous, Paul?" Vivian asked.

"Because your husband's going to scratch Willie if it rains, and I don't see how it can hold off a minute longer."

"He's not going to take him out of the race," Vivian admonished. "In fact, make sure you bet him because he's going to win for fun."

Mrs. Farrington, who had bet small sums on Willie in the past, could not bring herself to wager on him that evening. In her mind, the Almighty had assured her that her pacer would win, and she felt it would be unfair of her to take advantage of that knowledge. But she had no reservations about passing the word on to her partner.

The rain, when it came, fell as it only falls in California—in giant sheets drenching everything within sight in seconds. The hard and dry loam of the Hollywood track quickly turned to soup. Seibert was astounded to see Rambling Willie come out on the track for the featured sixth race, and looked on with wonder as Farrington limbered him up briefly, then steered him to his assigned post behind the starting gate.

All of Willie's fiercest rivals—Nero, Momentum, Young Quinn, Tarport Hap and H.A.'s Pet—were in the rich affair, but it was no contest at any point, at least not for the win. Farrington sent Willie into a quick lead and never looked back, pacing through the slop in 2:02 1/5 and winning by three open lengths.

"I'll be damned," Seibert muttered as he and Vivian sailed down the stairs, heading for the trophy presentation.

"How much did you bet on him, Paul?" his co-owner asked as they arrived on the ground floor.

"Bet on him? Nothing. Hell, I was convinced he wouldn't race."

"Paul," Vivian sighed, "I've told you a thousand times, you've got to believe."

"Starting now," Seibert shot back.

"It's a little late, isn't it?"

"Late? No, it's not late. Willie's not done for the season. He's got a few races left. I've still got time to get rich."

"Or poor," Vivian added, chuckling.

Chapter 14

*T*he fifteen days before Christmas rouse traditional emotions in most Americans, simple pleasures shared by family and loyal friends. For harness horse owners and trainers the season awakens an added excitement.

As an entire nation scurries about buying gifts, mailing cards, planning parties and dialing distant relatives and friends, the sport anticipates one of the most treasured customs of the yuletide—announcement of the Horse of the Year awards.

The annual proclamations are the standardbred industry's Academy Awards, top ten poll, Pulitzer and Nobel prizes all rolled into one. The honors are determined by a plurality of the nation's harness writers. They are hotly debated by the losers and deeply cherished by the winners. The awards become the perfect gift for a horseman's Christmas stocking.

The top honor in 1976 went to a spectacular three-year-old pacer named Keystone Ore, world champion winner of well over a half-million dollars, two legs of Pacing's Triple Crown and more two-minute miles during a single campaign than any racehorse before him.

It was near impossible for an older horse to deprive a younger foe the Horse of the Year crown. The structure of the sport and its publicity machinery were geared to lionize, *exalt*, the junior competitor.

Rambling Willie—twice the age of Keystone Ore—was the writers' preferred choice as Aged Pacer of the Year for the second straight season. His world records, dozen victories in twenty-five starts, all-time single season earnings record by a gelding of $295,750, and continued rule over the nation's most seasoned pacers pegged him as the logical choice.

His late-season flourish following his miraculous recovery from the bowed tendon secured Willie many emotional votes. He was not languishing in a stall as the experts and the odds predicted. Instead, he won two of his final four starts of the year, including a gritty 1:56 1/5 win at Hollywood Park and a 1:57 3/5 winter racing record mile at New England Harness Raceway in Foxboro, Massachusetts. There were a few disappointments in the months following Willie's bow—specifically the gelding's failure to win Hollywood Park's American Pacing Classic, one of the few rich and classic races for free-for-all pacers that had continued to elude him—but they could not cloud his incredible courage and unflagging vitality. Logic aside, Rambling Willie was the writers' sentimental pick.

The public relations men at the U.S. Trotting Association were not blind to Willie's magnetism. News of his award was unveiled with a bit more dash, a snip more splash, than even the announcement of Keystone Ore's title.

Facts, figures and quotes detailing Willie's big-hearted work for the Lord escorted the standard release of his racing record to the desks of the national press. When the news had been first planted with the media in the Spring of 1976, the effort by the USTA publicity team had harvested a bumper crop of headlines. This time, the salvo of information fired at the newsmen created an enormous explosion.

It seemed whenever a sportswriter or sportscaster tired of the tedious on-again, off-again love match between tennis stars Chris Evert and Jimmy Connors, or the ceaseless off-season banter and boasts by top-dollar athletes on the subjects of salaries, teammates and trades, they filled their columns or shows with the saga of Rambling Willie.

The possible variations for packaging the facts were infinite:

Consumer News—"Someone has been working like a horse to pay for improvements that have been made to the Church of Christ in West Mansfield. . . . Not only has the generous contributor worked like a horse, but he is a horse."

Sports Illustrated—"Harness racing is getting on the side of the angels."

Chicago *Sun Times*—"The Rev. C. L. Harris is not a fan of

horse racing. But it's forgivable if he says a small prayer occasionally for a certain pacer."

The National Star—"A tiny Midwest church is keeping its head above water thanks to the tithe it receives from its biggest benefactor—a champion harness horse."

Bellefontaine, Ohio, *Examiner*—"One of the most famous and active participators in the West Mansfield Church of Christ never makes it to church on Sunday. Mostly he hangs around race tracks."

The National Enquirer—"The pastor of a church that frowns on gambling includes a racehorse in his daily prayers—because the winnings of Rambling Willie, 'the tithing horse,' help finance the church."

The Cincinnati *Post*—"The good churchfolk of Logan County are praying Rambling Willie has another great year in amassing earnings on the nation's race tracks. The six-year-old pacing gelding has garnered more than $600,000 in purse earnings during the past three years to lead all 'aged' pacers in the U.S. and is reverently known around here as the 'tithing horse.'"

The Lima *News*—"The Rev. C. L. Harris isn't a diehard horse racing enthusiast, but he has good reason to follow the fortunes of one pacer."

If the prophet Malachi had intended to repeat his gospel of the tithe in today's world, he could not have hoped to find a more conspicuous agent to demonstrate the benefits than Rambling Willie.

But in the normally peaceful village of West Mansfield, Ohio, the heirs to all the unexpected attention were distressed. They did not view the prodigious publicity in heavenly terms. The ink afforded the story was beginning to stain and strain the unique alliance between Rambling Willie and the West Mansfield Church of Christ.

The first suggestion of frayed nerves and discontent surfaced at a church board meeting. One of the elders produced a copy of an out-of-town newspaper story attached to a letter from a former church member. The woman blasted, *denounced*, the congregation's acceptance of Rambling Willie's tithe, cursing it as the work "of the devil and that's what the whole thing was going to end up with."

Her words produced a heated discussion. For the first

time, Willie's money had been challenged. Most of the elders and deacons still maintained that the money spawned from the livelihood of Robert and Vivian Farrington, that the matter was being blown out of proportion. A few of the more inflexible members lamented the whole business, trotting out the words "obscene" and "notorious" to drive home the point.

"Gentlemen, the Bible doesn't mention a single thing about gambling," Reverend Harris reminded his board. "We're all personally against it. But the horse's money is his whether anybody bets or not. Suppose we were dealing with a baseball player instead of a racehorse. Because people bet on ballgames, would we argue his tithe?"

"We must answer the letter, apologize for the publicity your daughter has brought us by her bragging," one of the more distressed elders said.

"Vivian never intended her tithe to be made public," Harris defended. "A friend leaked the story to the press. We have never uttered a single prayer for the horse. We have no reason to be ashamed. His picture was hung on our notice board . . . a sign of our community's interest in racing. Some of our members follow the horse's career; that is their private business. They aren't doing anything wrong.

"Why not be grateful for the good that can result?" Harris asked. "Someone may read the story and be changed by it. We never challenged the money when it only amounted to a few thousand dollars. Because it's now into the tens of thousands, it's no different. Nothing has changed. You know, they found fault with Jesus, too."

The majority of the board agreed with their pastor. A single letter was no cause to overreact. It did not outweigh the blessings the money had brought the church. The congregation at West Mansfield had not faced the financial woes afflicting neighboring churches. They had not lost a single member since the money began flowing into their treasury.

Nor had the windfall affected the charity of the other members. They understood Willie's money would not continue indefinitely. Their traditional support of the church's financial needs testified to the continued belief in self-reliance. They weren't banking on any free rides.

Instead, their aging church building had been remodeled throughout. New carpeting. New pews. New paneling. A new baptistry. A new sidewalk out front, a blacktop parking lot out back. New furniture. Three new Sunday School rooms. Increased church tithes to neighboring congregations and missions. A new bulletin board. A manicured garden. An assistant minister.

The church had even added a new roof. And God had not seen fit to send it crashing down on top of them.

The board was willing to ignore the matter—the controversial letter—for the time being. They were relieved when other letters did not follow. But, then, they were never told about the mail delivered to their minister's Rushsylvania home.

The number of letters eventually totaled about a hundred, the opinions of the writers split down the middle. Half the correspondence reflected the sentiments of an Oxford, Alabama, man who wrote, "Could you accept money from a house of prostitution or money from a moonshine operation?" Others were more flattering, certainly more tolerant. "If a guy works at a printing press all day that produces Bibles but has a dirty mind, that certainly doesn't make his money any cleaner," offered a past president of the North American Christian Convention.

A couple of letters, presumably written with tongue-in-cheek, arrived from neighboring ministers complimenting Harris on his daughter's devout faith. And asking where they might find their own Rambling Willie.

Harris blamed much of the controversy on the jealousies of less-fortunate churches and self-proclaimed guardians of the gospel. After all, he reasoned, God intended for people to tithe. The Lord never lied. The church's good fortune was simple evidence of the words, "Bring ye the whole tithe into my storehouse . . . see if I won't pour you out a blessing that you'll not have room to receive." It was God's *own* deal.

Harris had hard evidence that the horse's story inspired people to good. Paul Seibert donated two thousand dollars to the West Mansfield church and once sent a sizeable sum of money to a Cincinnati church after reading of their financial troubles. Other horse owners had written Vivian. They told of having been inspired to tithe their own horses' earnings. There were also letters from people of other professions wanting to tithe a portion of their income to Harris' congregation, though he always attempted to steer their charity to local parishes.

But, at the same time, the publicity Willie brought to the church began to inconvenience and annoy the private lives and worship of the one hundred and twenty members of the West Mansfield Church of Christ. Barely a week passed when some reporter didn't have another question, when a photographer wasn't occupying the time of their pastor with one more picture in front of their sparkling white church.

The camel's back was broken when a newsman acquired the names and addresses of each member of the twelve-man church board. He visited each of their homes, asking his questions. What he could not learn from one, he wheedled out of another. Some of the information was accurate. Some was not. The 1976 church budget was $16,000; Willie was the largest contributor at $14,800. That was fact. The church had built a gymnasium for their youth. That was fiction.

All of it was disconcerting. Much of it was incorrect. The whole affair was taking on a circus air, and the board members felt the congregation—themselves included—were the performing clowns in the center ring.

They met again in May to reassess the tithes from Rambling Willie and the storm of ill-feeling it had created.

It was enough. They were weary of the stares, disturbed by the many half-truths they read. They agreed with church treasurer, Francis Fogle: "Nobody wants to tell our side of this thing."

That being the case, the board unanimously voted not to talk to any more newsmen on the subject. They advised their fellow worshipers and minister to do the same.

When the decision was made, Rambling Willie was beginning his 1977 season. His success and well-being were still on many of the church members' minds, but for the first time in their five-year relationship with the horse, his name was hardly mentioned within the confines of the church. And then, only in whispers.

Chapter 15

The sight of a horse immersed in water up to his neck might startle the average person. Assuming the worst, the scene could be downright horrifying.

But as Bob Farrington stood at the side of the pool at William McEnery's Lockport, Illinois, farm, he was unperturbed—bemused, if anything—as he gazed at Rambling Willie plowing through the water, his legs pumping away in a perfect dog paddle, his raucous snorts causing his upper lip to curl, leaving him with a sort of toothy grin on his long face. Groom Mike Martin held him by a lead shank, guiding the half-ton swimmer around the pool.

The swimming of horses is a fairly recent innovation in harness racing, a training tool designed to condition trotters and pacers without risking their fragile limbs over the sometimes pitted, unyielding surfaces of training tracks.

Farrington, always a pioneer among his horse training peers, had learned the art in California several seasons earlier. He had practiced it out there, reaped rewards from it, and vowed to have his own pool when he built his new farm.

The Farringtons had wearied of maintaining a permanent home in Richwood, Ohio, and spending most of the year in the Chicago area, occupying a rented home or apartment. Now they were building a farm on forty-two acres of flat, prime, Illinois countryside, some fifteen miles southwest of Chicago. The horse swimming pool would be the centerpiece of the new complex when it was completed. Meanwhile, Willie was living at the McEnery farmstead and taking his daily laps in the McEnery pool.

It was late March, and Bob had driven the seventeen miles to the McEnery farm to arrange Willie's transfer to Maywood Park, where he would begin final preparations for his sixth year at the races.

Farrington was waiting to chat with McEnery as he watched his pacer clamber up a ramp and emerge from the pool, wiggling, wriggling and shaking himself like an oversized dog.

"Old fella looks fit, don't you think?" McEnery inquired as he shook hands with Willie's trainer.

"That he does," Bob agreed, nodding. "Time now, though, to get him up to Chicago. Got to get him sharp for the Maywood Pacing Series."

"He'll knock 'em dead," McEnery predicted.

"Well . . ." Farrington hedged. "I hope he's gonna be all right. But you got to remember, he had an awful time with a throat infection last October. And, of course, he bowed that right leg twice during the year. Them old pins have taken an awful beating over the years."

"Yeah, but he's tougher'n barb wire."

"Always has been. Been battling the best there is for years. Seen a lot of young hotshots come and go. But he's seven now, and he can't go on forever. I suspect I'll have to take it a bit easier with him this year."

"Wish I had your problems," McEnery quipped.

"Wish I had your confidence," Farrington laughed.

Willie arrived at Maywood Park on April 2, jogging and training for eighteen days before racing in a qualifying event. It was a raw, damp, grim looking day, but Farrington's pacer seemed not to notice as he left six outclassed foes fourteen lengths back up the track, pacing the final quarter in a bristling 28 4/5.

Vivian Farrington, watching his performance from the paddock fence, was ecstatic, fairly bubbling by the time she caught up to her husband and her horse. "Still got his wallop, hasn't he? Fast as ever! Bob, imagine what he'll do at The Meadowlands this year? Maybe win that new series. What do they call it, The Driscoll . . .?"

"*Vivian*," her husband interrupted soberly, "slow down. You're all keyed up because Willie scored a flashy win in a qualifying race. But, Honey, you know he was beating second-raters, green horses and old cripples. To win the Driscoll and races like that this year, he's going to have to beat class—Oil Burner, Armbro Ranger, Dream Maker, Silk Stockings, Meadow Blue Chip, and horses like that."

"I know, Bob. But you know me, I've got to have a goal."

"Viv, you want to have a goal, make it beating Warm Breeze. In my mind, whipping Lloyd's horse would make a season for us."

Warm Breeze was the property of Lloyd Arnold, Bob's former partner during the big years. He was the best of the yearlings bought by Arnold when he and Bob's brother, Richard, had left the Farrington fold in quest of Grand Circuit glories. Whatever disappointment and rancor that had existed when the two departed had long since washed from Bob's mind, but that didn't stop him from longing to hang a defeat on their star pupil with Rambling Willie.

Warm Breeze, somewhat in the mold of Willie, had become a great horse despite an affliction that had ended the careers—and often the lives—of hundreds of other horses. Breeze had not only survived the wobbles, a rare and deadly disease of the central nervous system, but gone on to become a champion at age three. After the Bret Hanover son won the 1976 Review Futurity at Springfield, Illinois, in 1:54 4/5, Arnold had become convinced that he owned potentially the fastest horse in harness history.

Lloyd Arnold, the man who used to race solely for money, was now interested in records, too. Arnold, by this time, included a track—Golden Bear Raceway in Sacramento, California—among his racing holdings. Bent upon setting a new track record—and perhaps a world record at the same time—he had imported, at great expense, an entire field of free-for-all pacers and top drivers for a record bid on August 1, 1976. Among the uninvited were Rambling Willie and Bob Farrington.

Jilley, a fleet sidewheeler handled by Lew Williams, had paced in 1:55 3/5 to crack the track mark, although the mile was far off the world standard. A year later, Arnold would send his own pacing star, Warm Breeze, after the world record and succeed.

Bob Farrington was prepared to admit that Warm Breeze possessed extreme speed and was a racehorse to admire. And he did not begrudge the success his brother and Arnold had enjoyed with the horse. But he felt it was high time that they tested their champion against his champion, Rambling Willie. Assuming, of course, that Willie still had his sting.

Willie's first engagements of the new season were in the Maywood Pacing Series, as planned. He finished third and second in the two preliminary legs, encountering bad racing luck in both. Sandwiched between the two losses was a heart-stopping nose defeat to Armbro Ranger, the salutatorian of 1976's class of three-year-old pacers. While defeat was always repugnant, Farrington was anything but disheartened by the three races. In each, Willie's strength, stamina and speed had climbed appreciatively, leading the trainer to believe that advancing age had again failed to take its toll on his wonder horse. He intended to test his notion in Willie's next trip to the starting gate.

The occasion was the $50,000 final leg of the Maywood Series, a contest that featured Willie and the three horses that had beaten him in his early starts—Kay Michael, Armbro Ranger and Keystone Accent. Farrington, ninety-nine percent sure his pacer was as tight and tough as ever, was almost unrelenting in his drive. He had Willie out battling from the start and never let up until he had the race clinched in mid-stretch. Then he let him coast to the wire, a three-length victor.

Bob was well pleased with the 1:58 2/5 clocking, knowing that it included a small vacation at the end of the mile. He was more pleased—*stunned* would be more accurate—the next week at Brandywine Raceway when his seemingly ageless pacing wonder polished off Town Drunk and world champion pacing mare Meadow Blue Chip in 1:56 2/5.

Only a nightmarish race at Yonkers Raceway, in which Willie was shoved all over the racetrack and had to scramble to finish third, spoiled his recent record as Farrington geared up for his horse's first head-to-head meeting with the friendly enemy, Warm Breeze.

Willie had won three of his last four when Farrington dropped his slip into the entry box for the $50,000 first leg of the U.S. Pacing Championship at Sportsman's Park on June 18. The Rambling Fury son was the defending champion in the annual series, a three-race affair held at three different tracks.

Warm Breeze, heading into the Championship leg, was

fresh off a 1:58 3/5 decision in the $108,750 American National Maturity Pace over the Sportsman's oval. He had produced three victories in his four starts on the 1977 season.

The Chicago fans seemed undecided as they began to pour their dollars through the track's pari-mutuel machines, but eventually settled on Willie as the slight favorite. It was impossible to tell whether logic or sentiment had guided them in their fiscal balloting, but there was no denying that Willie had long been a favorite son candidate in the Windy City. Included in the huge sum bet on the race were sizeable wagers by Paul Seibert and Lloyd Arnold, confident supporters from the opposite camps.

Cordiality was the hallmark of the pre-race chatter in the paddock, with Seibert and Arnold exchanging compliments and the brothers Farrington, Bob and Dick, swapping wishes of good fortune. An eavesdropper would never have guessed the intensity of the rivalry that existed between the two camps.

The race itself was an old fashioned donnybrook, although the two-horse showdown, the great confrontation, was anticlimactic at best. Willie left from the advantageous one-post, but could not beat the speed-crazy Keystone Accent to the lead. Farrington settled him back in third, but brought him off the rail and began the chase early when Keystone Accent, showing rare control, began to slow the pace. Approaching the half they were head and head—Willie on the outside—and Farrington knew he would have to keep the pressure on if he were to wilt his flying foe.

As the pair sailed past the three-quarters, still racing like a team, Keystone Accent suddenly capitulated, breaking stride. Rambling Willie and Bob Farrington had the lead to themselves, but Farrington knew the contest was far from over. Heading into the stretch, he heard a horse coming on, closing the gap, and figured it was Warm Breeze. He tattooed Willie's saddlepad with his whip, let loose with a loud and guttural "Haaa!" and hoped for the best. His pacer, pulling the effort out of his reserve tank, roared home at a 28 4/5 clip to preserve a length decision.

Farrington glanced to his right and discovered the horse that had been challenging him was Dream Maker, not Warm Breeze. Then he noticed that Whata Baron had finished third. Surprised, he looked back to the pack and discovered his brother's colors. Warm Breeze had finished fourth.

Bob knew that Willie had gone the toughest journey of the lot, parked out the better part of three quarters. Breeze, he also knew, had enjoyed a less-harried trip. Which meant, he figured, that his $15,000 Rambling Willie was a much better racehorse than Lloyd Arnold's $72,000 Warm Breeze.

A week later, in a carefully orchestrated world record bid at Arnold's Golden Bear Raceway, Warm Breeze paced a mile in 1:53 1/5 to become history's fastest harness horse in a race. It was a gargantuan accomplishment, hailed by the sport. But when Bob Farrington heard the news, he told Paul Seibert, "If Lloyd's horse went in 1:53 and a tick out there, Willie would have shaded 1:52." And he was serious.

Logic told Farrington that a seven-year-old horse with more than one hundred races behind him should not be improving. Yet Rambling Willie, thumbing his long nose at time, defying every rule of nature, was faster, a better racehorse at seven, than he had been at ages three, four, five or six. There was no denying it; the point was hammered home every time Farrington hopped into the sulky behind Willie.

Bob was a religious person, a man who practiced the Golden Rule and believed in the Almighty, but he was not in the same league with his wife. If he ever read the Bible, it was because the volume had been left open on the table, and his eye caught a phrase here and there the way an inveterate reader will peruse the label of a bottle of catsup. A practical individual, he had serious doubts that Vivian's prayers had healed Willie's bowed tendons, or that her tithing had kept the pacer racing so long, so well. Yet, being a practical individual, he also knew that *something* was keeping the old codger going, and he wasn't prepared to hand carte blanche credit to veterinary science.

He had to admit that an aura of religion, of faith, of the Bible, seemed to permeate the Willie camp, seemed to touch the horse at all times. On two occasions, he'd approached Willie's stall in the afternoon, after the day's training was over, and stumbled onto Mike Martin sitting in the doorway reading the Bible aloud.

"What in the world are you doing, Mike?" he'd asked gently, trying to hide his surprise. He had known Mike for years now, knew that he enjoyed parties, girls, and a good time. He had not known the young caretaker to be particularly religious.

"Reading the Bible," Martin said, voicing the obvious.

"Aloud?"

"Reading to Willie," the groom explained, grinning sheepishly.

"He like it? Does he pay attention?"

"Seems to."

"Well . . . you ought to keep it up, then," the trainer advised lamely.

"Going to," Martin commented. "Makes us both feel good, especially when old Willie's got a problem."

Later, driving home, Farrington had replayed the scene in his mind, shaken his head, and muttered, "Viv's influence."

Vivian Farrington had been quick to point out that Willie had zipped past their original goal—beating Warm Breeze— with relative ease. And with months left in the season. "We've got to readjust our sights," she counseled. "Let's win that big Driscoll thing at The Meadowlands."

"The Driscoll's a four-leg series against the top pacers in North America," Farrington pointed out. "Let's just plan to do as well as we possibly can."

"I'll agree to that," Vivian said obligingly, but added, "As long as we win the final leg."

Bob was looking forward to the Governor Alfred E. Driscoll Pacing Series. The Meadowlands, in its second season, was already one of his favorite tracks. The management treated horsemen the way they had always yearned to be treated, and it was an excellent place to earn a new speed record for your horse. Willie had lost his all-age world mark for geldings—a six-year-old gelding named Shadyside Trixie had lowered it to 1:54 3/5 in a race at The Meadowlands while Willie was racing in Chicago—and Farrington was itching for a chance to reclaim it. The world standards for aged geldings over half-mile and five-eighths mile tracks were still in Willie's portfolio.

A broken bone had eliminated Shadyside Trixie from the entire Driscoll series, but his presence was hardly missed in the opening race on June 30. Joining Willie in the $50,000 affair were champion race mares Silk Stockings and Meadow Blue Chip, fierce four-year-old champions Armbro Ranger and Oil

Burner, and a sprinkling of hard-knocking, free-for-all veterans like Le Baron Rouge and Town Drunk.

So tough was the field that Willie was on the oddsboard at four-to-one, the longest price he had offered in a year.

The Meadowlands crowd saw Rambling Willie lead the field down to the quarter in a sizzling 27 3/5 before surrendering the pace-setting honors to Oil Burner. Fly Fly Solly and Keystone Accent promptly took shots at Oil Burner, with the three of them motoring past the half in 56 seconds flat and the three-quarters in 1:25 2/5. Like a vulture, Willie pounced as the weary front-enders began to melt. He was past Fly Fly Solly, past Keystone Accent, and soon had Oil Burner headed. Willie had to hold off a fast charging Le Baron Rouge near the wire, but blasted the electronic beam with a good length to spare.

Bob Farrington, one of a rare few drivers who disdained the use of a stopwatch in a race—the clock was in his head—was aware that Willie was earning a life record in the race, and turned quickly to learn that new record on The Meadowlands' giant matrix board. He hooted happily as he read 1:54 3/5, aware instantly that his horse now shared the world mark with Shadyside Trixie.

The Red Man had a reputation to uphold—taciturn, unemotional, modest—but he had to strain to preserve that image in remarks to the press after the race. With a poker face threatening to explode with pride, he allowed that there were "several horses in the race that could have won with the trip Willie had. The horse that gets the breaks will win these Driscoll legs," he added.

The next day, shopping in New York City, he took Vivian into one of Fifth Avenue's best jewelry shops and ordered a diamond necklace with 1:54 3/5 emblazoned on it.

The Farringtons and their friends were forever ordering items, from expensive jewelry to plastic trinkets, to celebrate and mark Willie's racing milestones. Rings, necklaces, pendants and bracelets were exchanged, while hundreds of pens, shirts, jackets and cigarette lighters, all bearing Willie's name, were purchased and handed out to commemorate his accomplishments.

It was fun to do, and Heaven knew—probably better than

anyone else—the Farringtons could afford it. Willie's life earnings now stood at $796,561, with more than $40,000 of it going to the Lord through Vivian's tithing and Paul Seibert's gifts to the Church of Christ in West Mansfield.

The second leg of the Driscoll was two weeks away, so Bob entered his pacer in the second race of the U.S. Pacing Championship, the series that had started at Sportsman's Park. This contest was at Roosevelt Raceway, and Farrington would have been better off giving Willie a week's vacation. The Rambling Fury offspring was caught in a chain reaction collision at the start of the race, was forced off-stride, and had to hustle at the end to claim fifth money. The mishap prevented him from defending the title he had won in 1976. Even with a win in the third and final leg, Willie could not accrue enough points to claim the championship.

Not that the Farringtons and Seibert minded that much. Bigger sugar plums, like those offered in the Driscoll, were dancing in their heads.

Willie rejoined the Driscoll gang at The Meadowlands on July 14. This time, however, it was Oil Burner blessed with the perfect journey, pacing in 1:54 2/5 and holding off the hard-charging Willie by a slender nostril in the $60,000 competition. A week later, the racing luck shifted to Meadow Blue Chip, with the mare winning the $75,000 event in 1:55 flat, Farrington's pacer flying home from sixth to finish third.

Three legs of the Driscoll, three different winners—setting the stage for the $186,000 finale. The Meadowlands couldn't have arranged a more dramatic wind-up had its publicity director, Sam Anzalone, written the script.

Even the unflappable Robert Farrington was growing butterflies in his stomach as the July 28 shoot-out approached. Rambling Willie had never chased a purse so grand. Neither had Farrington. The owners of the winning horse would pluck $93,000 out of the $186,000 pot.

It was enough to push prospective winning owners to prayer, and Vivian Farrington led their prayer session in the Farrington's motel room before the race. Vivian, as always, was on her knees, while Bob, head bowed, sat on the bed and Paul Seibert occupied an overstuffed chair, feeling less self-conscious than he feared he would when his partner had first proposed the session. Each was lost in her or his own reverie, silently considering the important race only four hours into the future.

Vivian Farrington knew better than to offer an outright appeal for Willie's victory in the Driscoll—that would be in poor taste, unfair, too insignificant a thing to bring to the Creator's attention. Yet, at the same time, she yearned to give him an edge in the race. Finally, as the silent minutes passed by, a pleasant compromise settled in her mind. *"Lord,"* she prayed, *"let the best horse win."* Content that Willie was the best horse in the field, she rose, smiled, and ended the session.

Moments later, Seibert's three sisters—Esther Meadows, Gertrude Ramp and Florence Pauline—were knocking on the door, laughing, buzzing, ready to go to the track. Seibert, win, lose, or dead-heat, was determined to make an *occasion* out of the big race. He'd flown his sisters out to the giant track in New Jersey to give them their first look at this famous horse. Hopefully, Willie would reimburse him for their expenses.

As the rich race drew nearer—only a half-hour away—the batch of butterflies deserted Bob Farrington's stomach and landed in Paul Seibert's. Paul could barely manage his filet mignon, finally pushing it away half-eaten.

Across the table, Vivian Farrington, with bliss, peace and confidence decorating her pretty face, was in animated conversation with Seibert's sisters. How in God's name can she be so unconcerned, Seibert asked himself, suddenly realizing that he'd answered his own question. It had something to do with God's name. . . .

Down in the paddock, Rambling Willie flung his head around nervously, making the metal cross-ties jingle, and pawed the earth. Bob Farrington, with his confidence growing with every warm-up mile, spanked the ground with his whip and waited anxiously for the call to post.

And then it was race-time as thousands of fans among the crowd of 25,883 surged to the fence, the white starting gate started in motion, announcer Ed Gorman began his sing-song chant, and a feeling of electricity whipped through the night air.

One minute, fifty-five and one-fifth seconds later, it was over. Everything that could go Rambling Willie's way, went Rambling Willie's way. Meadow Blue Chip, frightened by a footprint on the track, jumped high in the air. Oil Burner was barely in contention. The rest of the entries ran out of steam chasing the uncatchable Willie. At the end it was Willie by three open lengths, $93,000 richer.

Vivian Farrington and the Seibert clan had no trouble reaching the winner's circle, Vivian and Paul having been there before. The circle itself was a maelstrom of shouting, laughing, back-slapping people—photographers, reporters, track officials, celebrities, and strangers.

Bob drove Willie carefully into the scene, the crowd parting to permit his arrival. He slid off the sulky, handing the lines to Mike Martin, heading for his wife and Seibert. A track security man reached to grab Willie's bridle, holding the lathered horse in place for the photo session. Bob had swapped bear hugs with his wife and Seibert, and shaken a dozen hands when he spotted a familiar face in the throng of well-wishers.

"Squeaky," he yelled, pounding Paul Sherwood on the back. "What the hell are you doing here?"

"Watchin' you win $90,000," Sherwood grinned.

"Man, I've been trying to track you down since Christmas," Farrington said. "Been trying to hang a thousand-dollar check on you for months. Now you stick close to us, 'cause we're heading into New York for a big steak dinner. And when we get there, Viv'll write you the check."

"Check? For what?"

"For what? For finding me *him*," Farrington said, dramatically aiming a finger at Rambling Willie. "For finding me the toughest, gamest, grittiest, best damn pacing horse the world has ever known!"

Chapter 16

In the days following Rambling Willie's swashbuckling victory in the $186,000 Final of the Governor Alfred E. Driscoll Free-for-All Pacing Series, the sport of harness racing was literally singing his praises.

The *Harness Horse*, a respected Eastern-based trade journal that had been reporting racing results and news on a weekly basis since 1935, wrote:

You sing, I'll play the music—Oh didn't He Ramble, Ramble, around the big mile track, never looking back—and that's the name of that tune . . . Not since Bret Hanover has a standardbred enjoyed such public acclaim and popularity. Willie sure does wow 'em.

The magazine's senior counterpart in the Midwest, *The Horseman and Fair World,* publishing since 1877, was less lyrical, more succinct, in its praises. The publication claimed the Driscoll win merited Rambling Willie a "solid claim for the *Pacer of the Year* award."

Few horses had ever evoked such kudos from the two conservative periodicals. But, then, few horses had exhibited the charisma or captured the imagination of harness rooters as completely as Willie.

Whether as a tribute to his talents, or simply an empathy with his common heritage and name, popular support followed the big bay wherever he went. Fans were enthralled by the seven-year-old gelding's vitality, his domination in a sport that usually paid homage to coltish competitors. Disciples of Rambling Willie's brand of "gray power" cheered as vigorously for his wins as they had for a field goal off the ageless toe of

George Blanda or a spitball hurled by the perdurable arm of Gaylord Perry.

When Willie loped onto the track at Freehold Raceway in New Jersey a week after the Driscoll final, 8,114 fans—more than double the track's average daily attendance for the year—cheered his win in the $30,000 R. Bruce Cornell Memorial Invitational Pace.

The victory marked Robert Farrington's first drive at Freehold since the early 1960s, when he had been the track's perennial driving champion, but the applause and chants of the crowd were mainly for Willie, not his driver, as the pacer notched a 1:58 triumph.

The following week at Greenwood Raceway in Toronto, owners of a rival horse competing against him in the $28,500 Beaches Stake underscored the captivating charm Willie possessed. During the final charge down the homestretch, with their pacer obviously beaten and Willie battling furiously to maintain a narrow lead over a late-charging Dream Maker, the opposition owners suspended loyalty and began to scream for Willie. As Dream Maker pushed his nose in front under the wire, the despair and disappointment at Willie's loss was written on the rival owners' faces just as it was on Vivian Farrington's or Paul Seibert's.

But racing fans at Greenwood maintained faith, and heralded the gallant gelding a racetrack hero's welcome by installing him an overwhelming three-to-five betting favorite the next weekend. Willie was bidding to become the first horse to string together three Canadian Pacing Derby wins with a score in the $86,500 feature. Beaches victor Dream Maker was after his second straight win as he took the field of pacers to the half-mile pole in a casual 59 3/5 with Willie resting in fourth. But half a mile later the order was reversed. It was Rambling Willie lowering Sir Dalrae's track and stakes records to 1:57 1/5, and Dream Maker back in the pack.

The pacer's popularity preceded him to the next Canadian stop—Rideau Carleton Raceway in Ottawa, Ontario. The crowd had read all week long about Willie's heroics and his charity. They had come to view him in the $20,000 Frank Ryan Memorial Pace, against the classiest collection of competitors ever invited to battle over the rural five-eighths mile racetrack.

His vogue pervaded the entire racing plant. The fans were primed to witness Willie's magic.

And he gave them all he had, racing three-quarters of the mile contest wide of the hubrail; all the while weaving through and around other horses. He was a far-back sixth going past the quarter-mile pole, seemingly hopeless in fifth at the half. Then he began the serious rush, up to third at the three-quarters and closing boldly down the stretch. But under the wire, the valiant effort failed by a head. Armbro Ranger was first, timed in 1:57 4/5.

Normally the upset of a big favorite electrifies a crowd, especially when the conqueror is a local native like the Canadian-bred and owned Ranger. But a strangely subdued crowd greeted Ranger as he ambled into the winner's circle, where the local racing secretary's wife and children were to present the race trophy. Most, including the young son holding the victor's prize, gazed off in the direction of the paddock where a glum Bob Farrington was inspecting his pacer, as if looking for the loose bolt or slipped gear that had cost the two the race. Back in the winner's circle, the disgruntled son with the trophy was reluctant to give it up.

"But Mommy, that's not Rambling Willie," he protested, pointing at Armbro Ranger. "I want to give the trophy to Willie."

Willie's star status was never more evident than when he shipped from track to track. When he traveled long distances, the headliner of the Farrington stable was awarded the VIP treatment of riding alone in an oversized van. The walls of the extra stalls were rearranged to form a single box-shaped enclosure, allowing the horse a small amount of movement.

When he was turned loose inside his paddock on wheels, Willie occasionally poked his head out an open trailer window to catch the wind against his face like an oversized family pet.

Willie was indulging in that pastime—his head protected from the cool winds by a red and white checkered hood—on his trip back to the United States following his three-week foray to Canadian racetracks. The sight of the masked gelding so spellbound one motorist that he drove his auto off the side of the road.

The van was headed to Brandywine Raceway, where Willie was scheduled to compete in the $40,000 General Mad Anthony. He was the richest—career earnings of $987,641—of the six pacers in the race, whose combined lifetime bankrolls totaled $2,332,413.

Anything short of victory would force Willie to wait at least another week to join the elite ranks of the sport's million-dollar winners. Getting to the prestigious plateau was like every other record Bob or his horses had approached under the watchful eye of an anxious and expectant sport; the pressures were intense, the reporter's questions nonstop.

"Coming off a loss to Armbro Ranger, do you think Willie can beat him in the Mad Anthony?" one reporter asked in a phone call that interrupted Farrington's dinner.

"Will you be doing anything special to prepare Willie for the race?" another newsman queried for his pre-race story. "How fast do you feel Willie will have to go to win? . . . How's Willie been training? . . . Is it true your wife tithes half the horse's earnings to a country church in Ohio? . . . What's it going to mean to have a horse that earned a million dollars? . . . Do you realize Rambling Willie never lost at Brandywine? . . . Where'd you buy the horse? For how much? . . . Did you know he'd be a great one from the start? . . . How'd the horse get his name? . . . If he wins the million, what next?"

The questions were still coming an hour before post-time. "Can the horse break the track record tonight?" a radio reporter probed as he shoved a microphone at Farrington in the Brandywine paddock.

"The horse went a bad race in Canada last week," a cautious Farrington answered. "I'm not sure what to expect tonight. I won't be after any speed records, just trying to earn a good check. We're in with a real tough bunch, and Willie might not be able to handle them."

The only answer that really mattered would come from Willie himself. As the horses approached the start of the race on the Brandywine backstretch, Bob seemed to sense that every one of the 11,042 people at the track had their eyes glued on his horse, their minds speculating what the aged pacer would do.

Finally, the starter gassed his gate and the race was under way. Armbro Ranger, Committeeman and Rambling Willie gunned for the lead. The first quarter was timed in a furious 28 seconds, with Ranger in front, Willie parked outside of him in second and Committeeman on the rail in third. Farrington continued to press his pacer toward the lead and grabbed it as Willie led the way past the grandstand on the five-eighths mile oval. He was in front at the half pole in 57, and still there at the three-quarter mile station in 1:26 1/5.

At the top of the stretch, Willie had a length advantage over Armbro Ranger. A final quarter-mile brush of speed, clocked in 28 2/5, increased that margin by another half-length. Willie was first under the wire, and the infield timer caught the mile in 1:54 3/5.

As surely as a painting bears the individual style of Leroy Neiman or a dress the distinctive design of Yves St. Laurent, this mile had the stamp of Rambling Willie all over it. He bettered his own world mark for geldings over a five-eighths mile track, set in 1975, by one and three-fifths seconds. He tied the all-age record set by two-time Horse of the Year Albatross in 1972, and equaled by the premier stakes-winning sopho-more pacing colt of 1977, Governor Skipper. The old track mark set by Oil Burner was lowered by two-fifths of a second.

In one brilliant effort, Rambling Willie had placed his name alongside the great French trotters Bellino II and Une De Mai, North American trotting champions Savoir and Fresh Yankee, and the elite pacers Albatross, Rum Customer, and Cardigan Bay as harness racing's million-dollar winners. In fact, his lifetime bankroll of $1,007,641 ranked him second only to Albatross among the pacers.

Even if Bob had entertained doubts about the horse's chances prior to the race, the management of Brandywine showed no such uncertainty. A sign, hailing Willie's millionaire status, awaited the two when they arrived in the winner's circle. As Farrington joyously tossed his whip into the crowd surrounding the winner's enclosure, he was amply reimbursed with a $1,500 check from track president Hap Hansen—bonus for breaking the track record. Then it was party time.

Drinks, hors d'oeuvres and small talk were served in the track's executive lounge. Farrington, his wife and her partner were the guests of honor, the trio that the press and friends of track management had come to toast.

One of the first compliments to reach Bob at the post-race celebration came from the radio reporter who had questioned him in the paddock prior to the race. "Don't think Willie can handle this bunch, huh?" the reporter joked, reminding Bob of his comment barely an hour old.

Willie had handled them all right, and Bob's hands still shook a bit from the excitement of his pacer's dramatics on the track. He knew full well that his horse was king and didn't mind telling the world—at least that portion that was within earshot.

"He went a super race," Farrington said. "The track was great, the weather was great, and the horse was great. Everything was perfect, and we took advantage of it.

"I'm forty-eight now and semi-retired," he continued. "Only drive about fifty races a year. Don't need any more with Willie around. He's the best thing that ever happened to me.

"And I won't let the old fella down. I won't spoil his record by keeping him going too long. When he lets me know he can't race with the best, that's it. I've got a nice paddock set aside for him at my Illinois farm. Willie's the best, and he's going to get nothing but the best."

Farrington had rarely been so effusive in his praise of any horse, but Willie was no ordinary horse. It was not his style to make the rounds of the Brandywine party like a movie star plugging his newest picture, but he certainly was available for any comments on his pacer that a reporter cared to solicit.

Neither Bob nor his wife, nor Paul Seibert was ready to put a cap on the evening when the last of the harness scribes and sportscasters headed off to file their stories. The Farringtons invited the dozen or so people left in the lounge to join them at the nearby Sheraton Inn, where the drinks were to be on Willie.

The festivities were into their second hour when Mike Martin, who had cooled, bedded and secured Willie for the night, arrived with a long-time friend of the Farringtons, Robert Seefeld.

Seefeld had worked as a caretaker for the Farrington stable when Willie began his early lessons at Maywood Park. A college graduate, Seefeld had moved to Philadelphia when he gave up his work with the horses, but had never surrendered his interest in Rambling Willie.

Seefeld made a beeline for his old friends as he entered the darkened bar. He had a kiss for Vivian and a bear hug for both Bob and Paul to commemorate their horse's newest honor.

"Where were you when we were having our picture taken in the winner's circle?" Vivian chided.

"Busy," Seefeld explained. "When Bob threw his whip into the crowd, I went hunting for the fella who'd caught it. Offered him fifty dollars on the spot. Would you believe he said he wouldn't take a thousand?"

"Damn inflation," Farrington kidded. "Listen, I got another whip just like it that I'll let you have for twenty-five bucks. I'll even autograph it."

"No thanks," Seefeld said, "But I'll make you a deal. Tonight was Willie's thirty-fifth two-minute mile. When he breaks Albatross' record of thirty-seven, you give me the whip and I'll pay you the full fifty."

Thirty-seven victories timed in two-minutes or better was a harness record that had endured since Albatross retired to stud in 1972. Robert Farrington suspected that of all the records Willie might set during his career, the two-minute mark was the most likely to survive.

Rich colt stakes, due to zoom as high as $2,000,000 for a single race at The Meadowlands, seemed to insure that some talented youngster would soon become a millionaire before outgrowing his colt years. As for speed, racetracks like The Meadowlands had already devalued the importance of fast miles, causing an upheaval in the record book. Famed trainer Del Cameron summed up the feeling in an interview in 1976, commenting, "Used to be, you had a horse that broke two-minutes, you had something to brag about . . . Nowadays, all you have to do is go out and claim one."

But Albatross' record was more than an example of a horse's occasional burst of speed or racing luck. To tuck thirty-seven miracle miles under a horse's harness required consistency and longevity. Farrington publicly admitted there were probably pacers faster than Rambling Willie, but he never expected to see one as consistent during his lifetime. Nor as enduring in the racing wars.

In fact, the difficulty of breaking the record was made painfully clear to Farrington during the final two months of Willie's 1977 season. The gelding inched within a single two-minute win of Albatross' standard twenty-six days—four races—after the General Mad Anthony. The event was a $15,800 affair at Hollywood Park, won in the time of 1:55 4/5, a track record for aged geldings at the California track.

But Willie was never able to earn the record-equaling two-minute trip that season. He started five more times—even scored three wins—but the closest he came was a nose loss to Oil Burner on October 8, timed in 1:56 4/5. That failure was one of two flaws in Willie's 1977 campaign.

His jinx in Hollywood Park's American Pacing Classic, one of the few major free-for-all races he had never won, was the second. Swelling and heat in his previously injured tendon forced Farrington to scratch Willie from the one and one-eighth mile test an hour before the horses headed for the post.

When news of Willie's withdrawal was announced to the crowd, it brought cheers from a group of rival owners obviously relieved that their horses had a better chance to grab the winner's share of the $110,250 purse with Willie on the sidelines.

Oddly enough, the incident had its pleasing side for Willie's backers. The show of poor sportsmanship particularly irked Paul Lavoie, proprietor of a Quebec City, Quebec, steak house and owner of a pacer in the Classic named Le Baron Rouge. Mortified by the misbehavior, Lavoie apologized to the Farringtons and Seibert. He also revealed that the story of Vivian's generosity had so touched his life that he had pledged a portion of Le Baron Rouge's earnings to charity.

In one of those familiar moments of poetic justice that seemed to favor the people in Willie's corner, Le Baron Rouge burst from the middle of the pack of pacers around the final turn and captured the victor's portion of the Classic purse by a nose at longshot odds of nine-to-one.

As for Rambling Willie, his season ended with thirteen wins, ten seconds and five thirds in thirty starts. His 1977 earnings of $397,921 was a single-season record for a gelding and raised his career take to $1,066,437.

Willie had visited thirteen tracks, ten cities, six U.S. states and two Canadian provinces in 1977. His vast accomplishments and limitless popularity had earned him a third straight Aged Pacer of the Year trophy, his third consecutive Ohio Horse of the Year award, and Illinois Horse of the Year honors.

As the veterinarians doctored Willie's leg, Americans were reading about his incredible season in the nationally syndicated column of Jim Murray. In a piece entitled, ''They're Praying for

Willie," Murray observed, "It's the kind of story Damon Runyon used to sell to the movies, and on which Frank Capra would win an Academy Award."

Unbeknown to Murray, his column—probably those very words—spurred a youngish Hollywood producer named Ken Wales to phone the U.S. Trotting Association's publicity department. He was toying with the idea of a feature-length movie based on the almost unbelieveable story of Rambling Willie and the people around him.

Only a handful of horses achieved national recognition from the non-racing oriented media that year—Rambling Willie, Triple Crown winner and thoroughbred Horse of the Year Seattle Slew, world champion and harness Horse of the Year Green Speed, and the three-time thoroughbred Horse of the Year Forego.

Willie and Forego were the oldest of the group, now late into their seventh years. Campaigning on uncertain tendons and ligaments, but with oversized hearts, they had earned the respect and admiration of a nation, a continent, and perhaps a world.

Forego had won thirty-three races in fifty-five career starts. For Willie, the box score read sixty-one wins in one hundred and thirty-nine trips to the post.

For six straight racing seasons, Willie had earned more money and a faster record than the year before. For his thoroughbred counterpart, the passage of time had not been so generous. Though Forego's victories continued, his seasons grew consistently shorter. In 1977, for the first time, his annual bankroll did not match that of Rambling Willie. In 1978 he would be forced to retire.

Soon, Willie would reign supreme—and alone—as the grand old man of horse racing. And the nation's news media, more than ever, would descend like a swarm of locusts settling on a Kansas wheat field.

Chapter 17

*W*hen the new insatiable demands of the media for cooperation in telling the Rambling Willie story clashed with the steel curtain of censorship imposed by leaders of the small, white-frame Church of Christ in West Mansfield, Vivian Farrington turned to the Arbitrator who had been helping her solve dilemmas all her life.

She sought the counsel of the Lord.

The pressure had begun in 1976, increased in 1977, and now, at the start of 1978, was reaching flood proportions, threatening to burst out of control.

In the past, it had been relatively simple to deal with men and women from isolated newspapers and smaller magazines, satisfying them with limited cooperation . . . shielding, as much as possible, her beleaguered father, the Reverend C. Lloyd Harris, the octogenarian pastor of the small church.

But now there were giants pressing for information— *Sports Illustrated*, *Time*, NBC's *Nightly News*, the Associated Press—and their representatives were high-powered, persuasive, demanding, not about to accept cursory explanations of the mystical aura that surrounded Rambling Willie.

And now a Hollywood producer—not the typical Hollywood filmmaker, but a religious person, the son of a pastor himself—was calling, proposing a wholesome, family-type movie based upon Willie and his coterie. And a pair of writers was knocking at the door, asking for her help in preparing a book-length biography of her famous horse.

No one had to tell Vivian that the new entries in the media

derby, some of them national institutions, would insist upon the total Willie story—the tithing, the prayers, the miraculous cures, the secrets of Willie's astounding racing longevity included. And she was aware that her father and the small church he served could hardly be spared, would have to be an integral part of that story, violating the rule of non-cooperation laid down by the church's lay leaders.

Vivian believed she knew the direction that God wanted her to travel, the road He wanted her to take. But she wanted confirmation. Not some elaborate, traumatic, earth-shaking vision, but a word, a simple sign, that would tell her He wanted the Rambling Willie story—all of it— to reach millions.

One night in March of 1978 she knelt by her bedside and asked the Lord to let her dream of horses if it was His wish that the saga of Rambling Willie be spread as far and as wide as possible—as an inspiration to others, as a lesson in what tithing and faith and prayer can mean to the practitioner.

That night an image of dozens of horses grazing serenely in an incredibly green pasture appeared so vividly in her mind that it woke her from sleep.

Skeptics, hearing of her experience, were quick to point out that she was the wife of a professional horseman and had been around horses most of her adult life. It would be unnatural, they said, if she did *not* dream of horses from time to time.

While the skeptics were free to believe what they liked, and free to make fun of her if they chose—she was used to that, prepared for that—there was no question in Vivian Farrington's mind that God had spoken, that God had made His feelings known.

And none in her father's mind, either. Lloyd Harris knew his daughter, knew of her all-abiding faith, knew of her adherence to the Golden Rule, knew of her long support of the church, knew of her ability to communicate with the Creator. And he knew her to be a modest person, an individual not likely to use her world champion horse for personal glory

Reverend Harris knew God, too, and had learned in six decades of service to Him that He sometimes worked in unusual ways. It was not outside the realm of possibility, Harris felt, that God would create a world famous racehorse, then use him to distribute His important message. After all, hadn't He used bread, fish, the sea, His only Son to demonstrate His power, to spread His word?

The reverend knew that God had constructed Rambling Willie out of genes, blood, organs, bones and muscles, just as He had fabricated all horses. But He had built Willie in such a manner as to make him outstanding among his peers, a champion among horses. And didn't the Bible advise, *"Whosoever will be great among you, let him be your minister; And whosoever will be chief among you, let him be your servant?"*

Couldn't Vivian's horse be a minister in harness, a missionary with sulky?

Both daughter and father were convinced that it was more than merely possible, that it was meant to be. The Lord, they believed, had intended Rambling Willie to be a messenger. And the Lord, they further believed, had intended them to cooperate with the media in order for Willie to serve as that vessel.

When Doug Looney, a writer for *Sports Illustrated*, requested in-depth interviews, they obliged. Reverend Harris sat for hours answering Looney's questions, providing him with a story brimming with color, wit, charm and simple faith. The story, because of its content, Looney's talent, and perhaps a touch of divine intervention, later won the John Hervey Writing Competition's grand prize as the best harness racing article of the year.

Dick Schapp of NBC's *Nightly News* arrived next, bringing a television film crew with him. Reverend Harris sat on his front porch chatting with Schapp, punctuating the filmed interview with gentle advertisements for religious tithing.

The Farringtons, Bob and Vivian, at their own expense, flew from Chicago to The Meadowlands, then brought a lame and ailing Rambling Willie up from southern New Jersey to enhance the filmed report. A tape of Willie's most recent race, an awesome come-from-behind win in the mud at The Meadowlands, completed it, giving Schapp one of his most talked-about television pieces of the year.

Reverend Harris, offering at least token compliance with his church's ban on publicity, declined to accompany Schapp and his crew to the West Mansfield Church. But he let it "slip" that a cellar door would be open to the building, permitting the crew to film the improvements that Rambling Willie had provided. Some of the church's parishioners, spotting the television people wandering in and out with cameras, reported that burglars were at work in the church.

Next on the scene was Ken Wales, the youngish Hollywood producer who had become enchanted with the Rambling Willie story and was determined to commit it to film, the money men of the film colony willing. Traveling with him were the authors of this book, intent upon extracting a pledge of cooperation from the Farringtons and Reverend Harris. Wales and his dream were welcomed, while the writers received their commitment.

Time, the Associated Press, and a raft of individual newspapers, some of them covering the Willie story for the second and third time followed, beating a path to Rushsylvania and West Mansfield, Ohio, and Mokena, Illinois, or keeping the phone lines humming between their newsrooms and those communities.

The Farringtons accepted every call, answered every question, posed for every picture. So did C. Lloyd Harris, dazzling every interviewer with his beaming countenance, his wry humor, his bouncy, time-defying energy, and his deep devotion to the Lord and his church.

And when the featured players in the Willie story were absent or unavailable, the subalterns—stable bookkeeper Steve Rosmarin and new caretaker Dean Collins—were urged to go out of their way to cooperate with the media, to respond to every query, no matter how silly or how probing the question. Neither Rosmarin nor Collins was deeply religious, but both had witnessed minor miracles in their limited days with Willie and were not reluctant to discuss them.

Collins, a very tall, very slender youth of twenty, had succeeded Mike Martin as Willie's groom. Martin had ended four years of close, intense, sometimes rocky stewardship over the famous pacer, leaving in January, 1978, to accept a job with a horse transportation company. The Farringtons viewed his departure with mixed emotions.

Bob had battled with the young groom on many occasions, calling him headstrong, and criticizing him— sometimes severely—for using wild, unproven concoctions on Willie's battered legs. But, Farrington had to admit, there had been times when the caretaker was right, the trainer wrong. And no one, certainly not Bob nor Vivian, had cause to doubt Martin's enormous affection for Willie. They'd seen his grieving face, heard his prayers, when Willie was suffering, when the pacer's racing career was seemingly ended. And they'd seen the two of them sleeping side by side in the stall or paddock, like a kid with a big, devoted dog.

The new youngster, Dean Collins, possessed many of Mike Martin's traits—the ardency to duty, the protectiveness, the spit and polish. But Dean was less volatile, more amenable, less inclined to grab on to flamboyant remedies for use on Willie. Bob Farrington had known Collins for some time and had been impressed with him while watching him work as a groom with the Gene Riegle stable. When Collins parted company with Riegle, Bob had quickly recruited him, earmarking him as the successor to Mike Martin if and when the latter decided to seek greener pastures.

Steve Rosmarin, the stable's big, bulky and bright accountant, who had preceded Collins to the Farrington operation, told the new caretaker flatly, "Bob figures you're the best groom in the outfit or there's no way you'd end up rubbing Willie."

But Collins, with due modesty, had already figured that. He was aware he was taking on a ponderous responsibility— Willie was the king, everybody knew that—but he was both flattered and happy to accept. The fact that the Farringtons had given Mike Martin one percent of Willie's earnings in lieu of the traditional caretaker's tip was not the deciding factor, but surely helped.

Collins, like Rosmarin, was instructed to oblige the press in light of Rambling Willie's new role as an ambassador of God and living example of what tithing could mean to the donor.

All the Willie crew—Vivian, Bob, Paul Seibert, Rosmarin, Collins and, certainly, the Reverend C. Lloyd Harris—quickly learned the prodigious power of the national press. The mail they received in response to stories carried earlier by individual newspapers and smaller magazines had been impressive. Now it was a torrent, arriving from every nook and cranny of North America.

Reverend Harris, innocently, had mentioned his home-made healing salve, the Balm of Gilead, to *Sports Illustrated* writer Doug Looney, and Looney had made it a quaint part of his Rambling Willie story. Suddenly, hundreds of orders for the balm came flooding in, swamping the busy pastor and draining local drugstores of some of the ingredients needed to manufacture the salve. The reverend's grandson, Don Ray of Chicago, had patented the medicine a year or so earlier, and a large pharmaceutical laboratory, reading the magazine article, was soon courting him, hoping to buy, produce and merchandise the product.

More importantly, the reverend and his daughter—especially Vivian Farrington—were receiving messages from strangers who had read, seen or heard the Willie story and had been profoundly affected by it. Some said they were considering tithing a portion of their incomes to God, while others indicated they had already begun. The notes brought a welcome, warm glow to Vivian and her father, reinforcing their decision to permit Willie to labor for the Lord as a sort of four-legged publicity agent.

There were crank letters, too, but they were in the minority. One woman, either missing or short-cutting the point of Vivian's mission, wrote a letter detailing the hard knocks life had dealt her, not the least of which was poverty. Since Vivian was obviously a practicing Christian, the woman reasoned, it made sense that there would be enough charity in her heart to give a portion of Rambling Willie to the writer.

Closer to home, an acquaintance phoned with a desperate plea for financial help. The acquaintance's husband was an alcoholic, had lost his job, and the couple was unable to meet mortgage payments on their home. Since the Farringtons had done so well, and since Vivian's horse had earned more than a million dollars, couldn't she see her way clear to loaning the family a five-figure sum to get it back on its feet?

Mrs. Farrington did not hesitate in turning the woman down, instinctively aware that a loan was hardly the antidote for the couple's problems. Instead, she recommended that the family read prescribed passages in the Bible, then pray together. The caller slammed the phone down in disgust.

Months later, Vivian saw the woman at a social gathering, a party involving dozens of persons. The lady was hovering about the fringe of the crowd, her eyes on Vivian, apparently waiting for an opportunity to talk with her privately. Finally, when the crowd had thinned, she approached, and Vivian braced herself for a scene.

"You know," the woman told her, "when I asked you for a loan and you suggested the Bible and prayer instead, I wrote you off as some kind of hypocritical religious freak. But I have to tell you, we actually followed your advice; there didn't seem to be anything else to do at the time. We read and we prayed, as you suggested, and do you know, it caused a dramatic change in our lives.

"My husband quit drinking, found a decent job, and all the stray pieces of our life together seemed to fall into place. *We're* into religion now, heavily and happily. We give everything we can to the church, and all our spare hours are devoted to helping youngsters in trouble, taking them into our home and teaching them Christian solutions to their problems. It's a joyous life now, and you're responsible. I only wish to God I'd had the courage to tell you sooner."

The tears were ruining the fastidious Mrs. Farrington's makeup, but she didn't mind at all.

Vivian saw it as another striking example of what faith, once accepted, was able to do.

Faith, of course, had always been the cornerstone of her rearing, and it had helped the Harrises to transcend disasters that might have broken the spirit of less believing families. Vivian herself, as a young wife, had been horribly injured in a car crash that had taken the life of another woman. Chuckie, the youngest of the Harris children, retarded to start with, had died, seemingly without rhyme or reason, after having his baby teeth removed. Bill Harris, Vivian's brother, had been stricken in the prime of life—at age thirty-two—leaving a wife and three children. And, then on February 9, 1978, the family's faith was tested again.

Bonnie Harris, the gentle loving wife of the Reverend C. Lloyd Harris, the mother of Vivian Farrington, died of cancer. Mercifully, she did not suffer long from the insidious disease, but her passing left two daughters, a son, and an eighty-six-year-old husband destined to live out his life alone in a house filled with knickknacks, mementos and memories.

But the aged servant of God refused to wallow in pity, to call it a life. His wife would not have wanted that, and neither, certainly, did God. Within days he was back at work in the corner market, back to making his healing salve, back to making his visits to the ailing, back in the pulpit.

His stoicism, his great faith, his smoldering desire to continue serving his church and Master, set the tone, the style for the entire family.

Soon, Vivian Farrington was back to spreading the word of God and tithing through that curious receptacle, Rambling Willie.

The Willie-Farrington team, after a prayer session led by Vivian Farrington, scored a stunning win in the $186,000 Driscoll Series Final at The Meadowlands in 1977. *Photo by Jim Raftery Turfotos.*

Below, Reverend Harris was under increasing pressure to avoid publicity involving Willie's role in the church.

Willie greets visitors while at rest in a Farrington paddock.

Below, Rambling Willie (4) rambles to victory on September 4, 1978, at Scioto Downs to increase his purse earnings to $1,210,662, an all-time record for a pacer at that time. *Conrad photo.*

Scioto Downs officials flank
the Willie team after the
veteran pacer soared past the
money mark. *Conrad photo.*

Vivian Farrington, posing here with granddaughter Gale Marie, received calls and letters requesting financial help.

Below, Rambling Willie holds off the field at Sportsman's Park to add another two-minute win to his all-time total—a record that experts predict will stand for years to come.

Bob was elected to both the Ohio and the national harness racing Halls of Fame in 1979. Driver Howard Beissinger joined him in the Ohio Fame Hall.

Below, Bob Farrington's ageless wonder (3) shocked them all when he captured the $40,000 first leg of the Driscoll Series at The Meadowlands in 1979. *Photo by Jim Raftery Turfotos.*

Right, it's great to be famous.

Bottom left, Willie, with his ears pinned back, looks his age, which was nine years at the time of this photo.

Bottom right, Reverend Harris was at work in the J and J Market in Rushsylvania, Ohio, when he suffered a stroke.

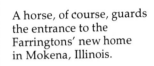

A horse, of course, guards the entrance to the Farringtons' new home in Mokena, Illinois.

Below, Bob Farrington, like the seemingly indestructible horse he raced, bounced back from severe back injuries.

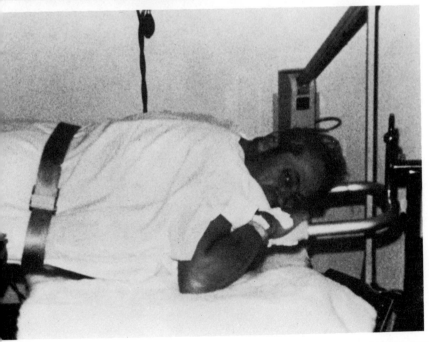

Two game veterans, Bob
Farrington and Rambling
Willie, return to the racing
wars at The Meadowlands.
Caretaker Dean Collins is
with them.

Chapter 18

*P*essimism, generously sprinkled with nostalgia, was the hallmark of Rambling Willie's seventh year of action in the racing wars.

It was, at least, for a major portion of the 1978 season.

"I know Willie can't go on forever," Bob Farrington told Jack Kiser of the Philadelphia *News* in May. "I know the day will come when age will do something no other horse has been able to do, to grab him by the throat and make him slow down.

"Hell, it's like asking a fifty-year-old man to outrace a twenty-year-old kid night after night," he pointed out to Kiser. "I know that one of these races he's going to tell me that the time has come to slow down . . . Just thinking about it makes me sad."

By June, the trainer was telling Rick Talley of the Chicago *Tribune*, "Actually, I think he has lost a little lick."

By July, he was confessing to Tony Sisti of *Newsday* that "Willie is slipping a little. His age is catching up with him and he's gone too many miles. I can't rough it up with him the way I could before."

His September message, passed on to Paul Keckstein of the Columbus *Dispatch*, was that Willie, sadly, had fallen "just a shade below the best now, can't quite reach back and give the really top horses the race he once did."

Throughout the interviews, the somber horseman was advancing the theme that he would be well satisfied if Willie managed to hold on long enough to snap the two key records held by Albatross; most two-minute victories by a standardbred, and most money earned by a pacing horse.

"That would make a season, even a career," he said wistfully.

While Farrington's assessment was certainly accurate, at least a portion of it seemed to be the product of his mind, not the aging legs or creaking joints of Rambling Willie. Or so it appeared to Willie's racing rivals.

Willie opened the campaign with a 2:03 victory in a qualifying race at Maywood Park on April 20, then returned a week later to score a leisurely 2:01 1/5 triumph over a classy corps of mutuel foes that included Fly Fly Solly and Taurus Bomber.

A scant three nights later, with a rocky flight from Chicago to Newark included in the package, harness racing's only active millionaire competitor took on the nation's best at The Meadowlands and turned them all away with a mile in 1:57 1/5.

It was his thirty-seventh two-minute win, tying him with the mighty Albatross.

Bob Farrington, with a cache of similar experiences behind him, was well aware that records have a habit of becoming highly elusive, downright slippery, when you're closing in on them, getting near enough to grab the brass ring. That syndrome was in force the next couple of weeks as Willie lost to Señor Skipper at The Meadowlands and bowed narrowly to Governor Skipper at Freehold Raceway.

Back on familiar turf—his luck improved. It was the $35,000 Paul Wixon Memorial, and Farrington was determined to remove the Albatross from his neck. He shouted and spanked Willie into an early lead, controlled the race throughout, and shook him up again at the end to preserve the decision over Goose Filter.

The time was 1:58 4/5, well under two minutes. Albatross' standard for miracle miles, set five years earlier, was the exclusive property of Rambling Willie. And every two-minute win that he would notch in the future would add to that mark, meaning his name was likely to remain in the record book for years to come.

The sport and its publications hailed the new king, but granted Bob Farrington no respite. When the racing journals were published the following week, one pointed out that "Willie is only $67,533 away from becoming the richest pacer ever, the next goal for the rugged veteran."

Farrington treated himself to a couple glasses of champagne and a large sigh, then made arrangements for his aged champion to fly back to The Meadowlands. Waiting for him, like a mugger in a dark alley, was a snarling new addition to the 1978 free-for-all pacing ranks, the resurrected Whata Baron.

Whata Baron was trained and driven by harness racing's top black horseman, the toothpick-slender Lew Williams. He was owned by Jeanette and Edward Freidberg, the latter one of America's most successful malpractice attorneys, a man who had made legal history by squeezing eleven million dollars in judgments out of a lone California surgeon.

Whata Baron, a six-year-old, had been bouncing around the fringes of racing's top classes since he was a three-year-old, winning a major race now and again, but hampered by a collection of ailments. Suddenly, in early 1978, he had blossomed like a poinsettia at Christmas time. He was now close to invincible.

Willie tried him on May 27, pacing a mile in 1:56 1/5 and still managing to lose by seven lengths. He tested him again on June 15, getting hopelessly caught in traffic and finishing far back. He tackled Whata Baron twice more—on June 22 and 29—paced a pair of dazzling 1:55 4/5 trips, but got no closer than five lengths to the Messiah of The Meadowlands, who set a 1:53 4/5 world mark in one of them.

It was with considerable relief that Bob Farrington learned trainer Williams was taking Whata Baron on the road, was embarking on a pilgrimage to several tracks in a Don Quixote-like attempt to set track and world records. It brought a broad grin to Farrington's face when word filtered back that Williams and the Freidbergs were retiring their pacer after a pair of unsuccessful bids in August to rewrite history over the fairground track at Syracuse, New York.

Willie's lone victory during that period was a 1:59 1/5 score in the mud at The Meadowlands on June 3. Mercifully, Whata Baron had been absent for that one.

It was highly unlikely that Rambling Willie would have beaten Whata Baron during the span had he been healthy; the Baron's ten-race win string being *that* overpowering. But Willie was hardly one hundred percent for the duels. Critics claimed factory-induced smog was fouling the air around The Meadowlands, presenting horses with throat and lung problems.

While Farrington was not about to get involved in that swirling controversy, he did know that Willie's throat was raw with virus, that his breathing was labored when he raced. It was a nagging thing that would bother him off and on for the balance of the 1978 season.

It was present, a faithful companion, as June turned to July and his trainer, increasingly frustrated, took him traveling in search of victories and cash. Willie was advancing on Albatross' money mark, but slowly, ever so slowly. He picked up $12,500 for a place finish behind Governor Skipper in his last Meadowlands outing on July 6. He earned another $6,000 finishing third to Big Towner at Roosevelt Raceway on July 15. Another $2,500 came his way for winding up fifth at Sportsman's Park on July 24, and a fourth place finish to Tricky Dick N. at Sportsman's a week later added $2,800 to his bankroll.

Heading into Toronto on August 26 for the $89,500 Canadian Pacing Derby—a race he had won three years running—Willie was $5,283 short of the $1,201,470 record. Finishing fourth in the Derby would send him over the top.

Typical of the sentiment riding with him was the draw for post positions, a ritual that took place three days before the Derby. Amazingly, some two hundred backstretch people gathered for the draw, and when a horseman pulled the favored one-post for Willie, the crowd cheered, whistled and applauded its approval.

The Toronto *Star*, as sentimental as the Greenwood horsemen, headlined its pre-race story, "The head says the Guv'nor (Skipper) but the heart says Willie."

Star sportswriter Dave Perkins elaborated. "In one stall on the Greenwood Raceway backstretch stands Governor Skipper, a marvelous looking, well-mannered four-year-old standardbred pacer, certain to be the betting favorite in tonight's $89,500 Canadian Pacing Derby. In the stall next door stands a chubby, snarly, thoroughly unmarvelous looking old man of eight named Rambling Willie. A lot of people are going to be cheering on the Governor, mainly because of their money. But nearly everybody will be pulling for Rambling Willie to do well tonight. . . ."

Bob Farrington, mired in gloom for weeks, told writer

Perkins that "Willie's still got one good move left. This is the first time in a while he's drawn an inside post. If he gets a good trip, he'll give a good account of himself."

However, the friendly post position did not help, and the "one good move" did not materialize. While Willie paced a decent mile—1:57 1/5—it got him no more than fifth money, $4,475, as the red hot Governor Skipper waltzed to a 1:56 1/5 victory.

Rambling Willie shipped out of Greenwood still needing $808 to snap the record.

When Farrington described the race to his aunt, Helen Farrington, he received an upbraiding over the telephone, rather than the consolation he was expecting.

"Are you sure you're not babying that horse?" Aunt Helen asked bluntly.

"Well, I'm being careful," Farrington admitted, flustered. "He's an old horse with lots of problems."

"Nonsense. He's the toughest of the tough," his outspoken aunt said flatly. "Now, take the wraps off him and get on with it."

"She could have a point," Bob conceded to his wife.

Farrington was weighing several offers from tracks drooling for Willie's services. He was only $808 short of the milestone, and almost sure of reaching it in his next start. The track landing the pacer was sure to earn itself some headlines.

Jim Ewart, the racing secretary at Scioto Downs near Columbus, was especially persuasive. "Look," said Ewart, "we're going to have a special $20,000 free-for-all on Labor Day afternoon, and it would be the perfect spot for Willie. Afternoon race, big and friendly Ohio crowd, not too many horses in the field. . . ."

"I don't want any gifts," Farrington protested.

"No gifts," Ewart interrupted. "I've got some pretty fair country pacers on the grounds, and I'll bring a couple more in to make sure you earn whatever you get."

"Sounds good," Bob agreed.

Farrington, dog-tired of the fuss his record hunting had created, was damnably anxious to have it over. At the same time, he abhorred the possibility of anyone or any track helping Willie to back into the record. Willie was a great horse and his trainer was as protective of his reputation as a mother badger is of her young.

"Win or lose, I'm going down the pike with him," he warned Vivian and Paul Seibert.

"Bob," Seibert pointed out reasonably, "you *have* to go down the pike with him if you're going to get a piece of that purse."

Indeed, racing secretary Ewart had done Willie no favors in assembling his Labor Day feature. Joining him were Missouri Time, the fastest aged mare of the year with a record of 1:56 3/5; Gleadon Creek, sporting a season's mark of 1:56 3/5; Quick Command, a 1:55 3/5 winner handled by Bea Farber, the world's best woman driver; Our Rebeck, a 1:56 3/5 victor at The Meadowlands; and New Deal, a seasonal winner in 1:58 3/5.

But Willie needed to beat only one horse to reach his goal. Fifth place was worth $1,000.

A flock of 8,812 fans turned out on a near-perfect afternoon to watch the racing fireworks, the chance to witness a small bit of history in the making drawing many of them. The late summer sun whipped down, its rays bouncing off the glistening backs of the six pacers as they rounded the clubhouse turn and were released by the starting gate on the backside of the five-eighths mile racetrack.

Farrington, bringing Willie out of the four-post, hustled him into second, then fell back to third as Gleadon Creek rumbled up on the outside to challenge pacesetting New Deal. The pattern was then set, with New Deal and Gleadon Creek head and head in the lead, and Willie third along the rail. They flashed past the quarter that way, then the half. At the three quarters, little had changed, except that Quick Command and driver Bea Farber had ranged up beside Willie and Farrington. Willie, fresh and full of pace, feeling to Farrington like a cobra poised to strike, was now effectively boxed in, blockaded, with no place to go.

Farrington waited for a horse to wilt, a hole to open, but none did. The field slammed into the final turn, with but an eighth of a mile to go, and nothing had changed. But, then, with two hundred yards remaining, a gap suddenly materialized. Farrington immediately filled it with Rambling Willie.

Shouts of "Will-eeee! Will-eeee!" a chant Farrington had

not heard lately, filled the air as he barreled through the hole, passing Gleadon Creek and taking dead aim at New Deal. Willie surged past the tired leader and swept under the wire with a length to spare in 1:57 2/5.

Rambling Willie was history's richest pacing horse, and he'd sailed past the old record with style, class and a victory. The $10,000 winner's share of the Scioto purse had boosted his career total to $1,210,622.

Hundreds of fans pressed against the fence as track publicity chief Chuck Stokes arrived with a neatly lettered poster reading, "Congratulations Rambling Willie, World's Richest Pacer, Scioto Downs, 1978."

Scores of people flooded onto the track to join in the celebration. Many of them Vivian Farrington had never seen before. Nor since. One woman, she noticed, was kissing Willie on the rump. Several more were slapping him on the back, like he'd just run a kickoff back for a touchdown.

Vivian searched the crowd for a familiar face and found one. She hurried over to hug her father, the Reverend C. L. Harris, whose tiny church had now netted more than $60,000 from Rambling Willie's racing heroics. She looked for Bob's Aunt Helen and spotted her, too. Helen had pushed her way through the happy throng to whisper in her nephew's ear, "I told you he was a tough son-of-a-gun." As Vivian watched, Bob's face creased with a grin and he began to nod vigorously.

The Scioto victory was like a new lease on life, the start of a fresh chapter in the saga of Rambling Willie. He journeyed to Hazel Park outside of Detroit and won there. He remained at Hazel the next week, wearing out his welcome as he won again. Farrington then sent him back to Sportsman's Park, where he met the best pacers in Chicago, and won again.

Willie did not lose again until September 30, when he got lost in a big field over a small track, the Yonkers' half-mile, marooned in seventh in a sea of horses arriving at the wire at the same time. On October 7, he paced a 1:58 2/5 mile over the same track to earn second money behind the same winner—Le Baron Rouge.

Willie's season, a campaign with all the stability of a twenty-five cent yo-yo, continued at Roosevelt Raceway, where, in a shattering reversal of form, he struggled to wind up seventh, thirteen dismal lengths the wrong end of Governor Skipper. The virus, an unwelcome guest that refused to leave, had him by the throat again.

Farrington was sorely tempted to call it a year, to send Willie back to the new farm in Mokena, Illinois. But two factors tilted his mind in the other direction: Willie's next start—the George Morton Levy Memorial Pace—carried a purse of $200,000, and Willie, who could heal faster than a character out of *Star Trek*, had apparently shaken his malady.

His trainer, back in the role of overprotective massa, started him with trepidation and raced him like he was a rare and fragile egg. When he finally turned him loose coming for home, Farrington discovered an awful truth: Willie was healthy, fresh and sharp. The Rambling Fury son made up six lengths in the short Roosevelt stretch, but could not dent the wall of horses spread across the track in front of him. He finished fifth.

"Hardly a vintage drive," he confessed painfully to Vivian and Paul Seibert.

"But he's healthy?" Vivian inquired.

"Very healthy," Farrington admitted, chagrined.

"We'll get 'em next week," Seibert interjected soothingly.

"You can bet on it."

"I will!" Seibert said, earning grins, shattering the gloom.

And he did, with Rambling Willie cooperating handsomely, defeating the best that Chicago's Balmoral Park could assemble in 1:58 1/5.

Every member of the Willie team—the Farringtons, Seibert, Aunt Helen, and caretaker Dean Collins—was ravenous for a triumph over Governor Skipper, and knew that November 17 would be their final opportunity. The Governor, owned by the Wirtz Family of Chicago, who also numbered the Chicago Blackhawks and the Chicago Bulls among their properties, was retiring, closing the book on a brilliant three years at the races. He was the latest—and easily the best—of the young upstarts to invade the free-for-all ranks after spectacular careers on the Grand Circuit. The Governor, in fact, had not only been named Three-Year-Old Pacer of the Year in 1977, but Pacer of the Year as well. The horse he had defeated for the larger honor was Rambling Willie.

"We haven't been able to do it all season, but I think we've got his number tonight," Willie's reinsman told Seibert in the Arlington Park paddock before the duel.

But a small disaster prevented it from happening. Willie had overhauled Governor Skipper at the three-quarter pole when his younger rival, with legs rubbery from a grueling season of mixing it with the free-for-allers, strayed off the rail and struck Willie's sulky. By the time Farrington had Willie righted, back to pacing up a storm, Governor Skipper himself and Le Baron Rouge had zipped by. The judges quickly set the Governor back in third for interference and put Le Baron Rouge's number up as the winner. Willie had to settle for second.

With November half over, the Chicago trees bare of leaves, the big races completed in the East, it was decision time again. Was it worthwhile to send Willie to California, where the $100,000-plus American Pacing Classic was scheduled, as usual, at Hollywood Park? Farrington, with some worry over Willie's questionable leg, decided in the affirmative. The horse was flown to Hollywood Park, arriving on a Sunday.

Willie was trained a mile and a half the following day and showed no ill effects. He trained twice more that week at long distances—an unusual load for the aged pacer—again without apparent pain or problem.

When the judges opened the entry box for the 1978 edition of the Classic, Rambling Willie was named along with thirteen of the greatest pacers still active in North America. Among the batch were Dream Maker, Le Baron Rouge, Senor Skipper and Sirota Anderson, all of them holding seasonal victories over Willie. The combined earnings of the fourteen exceeded $5 million.

The American Classic, as usual, was contested at a mile and an eighth, not Willie's favorite distance. At eight years, he was the oldest competitor in the field by far, giving away five years to some of his opponents. Despite such drawbacks, the folks that had managed his training pegged *him* as the horse to beat.

Roughly half the 15,000 Southern California fans in the stands, the clubhouse and on the ramps, agreed, sending Rambling Willie away as a sort of half-hearted favorite at odds of two-to-one. Enhancing his chances was the fact that Flight Director, one of 1978's swiftest three-year-olds, had been a late scratch, the victim of an ankle injury.

Bob Farrington, the rough and tumble driver from Chicago, the former national driving champion, was resolute in his desire to avoid entrapment in the herd of thirteen pacers, so he left fast and hard with Willie, grabbing the lead, then willingly surrendering it to a longshot called Try Scotch. He was now in the garden spot—the two-hole along the rail—purring along with his horse, hoping fervently that the eleven foes behind him would let him enjoy that advantage for a while.

On they went, down to the quarter, over to the half. Farrington could sense, then hear, activity behind him, but still no horse edged up beside him. He carried no stopwatch, but knew that Try Scotch was rolling along at a frantic clip, one good reason for the lack of challenges.

It can't last, he told himself, as Try Scotch, stalked by Willie, whipped past the half-pole in 57 2/5 and thundered on. They've got to be out and coming soon, he thought, or this ancient-but-noble animal I'm steering is going to steal the American Pacing Classic.

With the striped three-quarter pole coming up on his left, Farrington knew he could wait no longer. He pulled Willie's right line, guided him carefully off the rail, and whacked him once. The tough old veteran, with a heart the size of the 747s in their landing approaches overhead, was almost a blur as he shot past Try Scotch, grabbing command of the race. He had two lengths on the field at the mile marker in 1:56 4/5, but the roughest part of the contest remained—the final eighth.

Two of them were coming now, and Farrington knew that one had to be Le Baron Rouge. The other, surprisingly, was Tender Loving Care, the lone filly in the field, and a three-year-old at that. But Willie's driver was too busy protecting his lead to admire the tenacity and spunk of the female. He was slapping the lines against Willie's side and hollering with all the voice that he had left.

It was then that the three long-distance training trips of the previous week proved the proper prescription. The years seemed to peel away, to evaporate, as Willie dug in, plunging down the final hundred yards like a colt with legs of newly forged steel, his muzzle seemingly screwed up into a sort of snarl.

Rambling Willie passed under the finish wire first. With a

length to spare. In 2:11 flat. He had added the American Pacing Classic to his roster of major wins, made the list impeccable.

Joe O'Brien, who had lost a drive in the Classic when Flight Director was scratched, had watched the race from the paddock fence. A member of harness racing's Hall of Fame, a horseman of infinite experience and talent, a man of few and of soft words, O'Brien turned to a caretaker standing beside him and summed up the Rambling Willie story in a sentence.

"That may be the greatest harness horse ever born," he said.

Fifty yards away, in victory lane, that opinion was being reinforced in another way. A California writer was pumping Bob Farrington.

"With the Classic, Willie's won every major race open to him," he observed. "I suppose you go for Savoir's North American money record next week, since he only needs $4,258 to become the richest American standardbred in history."

"Won't be any more records this year," said Farrington. "Willie's lame."

"Lame?"

"Lame. He was sore on his tendon earlier in the week, and I can tell he's hurting for sure now. Got to quit with him."

"You mean to say he just beat the best pacers in the world at a mile and an eighth and he's not one hundred percent?" the reporter queried, stunned.

Farrington shrugged. "That's Willie," he said.

Indeed, it was a lame horse that left Hollywood Park and a lame horse that was unloaded at the Farrington's Illinois farm a few days later. As Rambling Willie's groom, Dean Collins, turned the animal loose in the football field-sized paddock reserved solely for the champion, he checked the blister—an irritant applied to a horse's sore leg to induce natural heat to hasten healing—he had placed just below the gelding's knee. It had been one of the cornerstones of cure for Willie's ailing leg, the stable's winter investment to underwrite his eternal durability.

Collins soberly watched as Willie slowly, almost tentatively, reexplored his wide-open space set between the Farrington home and stable office. Soon the hitch seemed to disappear from Willie's walk as he began to pace along the paddock fence. About twenty-five yards down his route, Willie came to an abrupt halt. He began to shake his head with a ferocity that seemed to express the sense of freedom he felt to be home again.

Suddenly, Willie raised his huge frame high in the air, balancing precariously on his hind legs as he pawed the crisp winter air. When he landed back on all fours, he unleashed a playful but powerful kick that demolished a lower slat in his fence.

Home had always had a recuperative effect on Rambling Willie. Collins was confident Willie would return for another season of harness heroics.

Chapter 19

*S*ome observers took a look at Willie's racing record for 1978 and pronounced him slipping. Still game, still tough, still a marvel, but slipping.

Granted, he had earned more than a quarter-million in purses—and contributed nearly $13,000 to the small Ohio church—but for the first time in his racing history he had failed to harvest more in racing spoils than he had the year before. In one hundred thirty-nine lifetime starts prior to the '78 season, he had fallen short of earning a paycheck (harness races offer a part of the purse to the first five horses in a field) only three times. In 1978 alone, the oldster had missed a payday in three of his thirty starts.

The slight slippage, however, had little to do with the fact that he missed election as Aged Pacer of the Year for the first time since 1975. Whata Baron, the sizzler who had hung four losses on him during the season, dethroned him, with fellow free-for-allers Governor Skipper and Big Towner rubbing salt in the wound by finishing second and third in the national balloting.

In the state of Ohio, where Willie had reigned as Horse of the Year for the past three seasons, he also fell from grace, but only by a whisker. A three-year-old pacer named Falcon Almahurst claimed the crown by a single vote, while actually deserving a more comfortable margin. Falcon had won the $750,000 Meadowlands Pace, picked up a total of $388,396 in purses, won a heat of the cherished Little Brown Jug, and time-trialed in 1:52 2/5. Sentiment had probably kept him from a clearer decision in the balloting.

If the year did not belong to Rambling Willie, it was the property of the man who patched up his wounds—more often with every passing season—and kept him on his merry rounds of America's harness race tracks. When Willie stepped to the wings in 1978, Robert Farrington moved to center stage.

Farrington's first tribute was induction into the Ohio Harness Racing Hall of Fame. He joined Howard Beissinger as the first inductees to be elected into the Hall, with enshrinement coming at a huge banquet in Columbus. His eulogists hailed his three hundred-win season, his six national driving championships, his three thousand-plus career triumphs, and the honor he had brought his native state. But when the discussion turned to horses, only one was named. The charismatic Willie.

Two months later, he had to dust off his tuxedo again and wear it at the Florida banquet of Harness Horsemen International, a country-wide confederation of horsemen's associations. He was HHI's "Man of the Year," with the proclamation praising his "immense achievements with Rambling Willie and the subsequent media coverage for harness racing, possibly the most positive exposure the industry has had in years."

Then, reinforcing the fact that Farrington and Willie had done a potent sales job for racing, the horsemen's group also named him honorary chairman of "The Race Against MS." The promotion was a union of HHI and the Multiple Sclerosis Society to raise money at harness tracks across the nation to fund the fight against the mysterious disease. Farrington's role was largely titular, but he did star in a nationally released television commercial, and a poster featuring him and a MS victim was distributed from coast to coast.

Willie's trainer welcomed the chance to help the less fortunate; he had been doing it all his adult life. But he much preferred to practice his charity in private. The man who had fearlessly driven harness horses for a quarter-century was admittedly petrified of a microphone. He enjoyed the limelight as much as the next man, but liked to earn his applause while seated in a sulky, not standing behind a podium.

His public appearances for the year had not ended, however. On Saturday, March 24, 1979, the U.S. Harness Writers' Association gathered at Hasbrouck Heights, New Jersey, to elect three new members into harness racing's Living Hall of Fame. The writers had inaugurated their Fame Hall back in 1961 with the election of E. Roland Harriman, who had "saved" the sport by preserving its records at a crucial time, and Stephen G. Phillips, the inventor of the mobile starting gate, as their initial inductees.

In the interim, twenty-five of racing's most illustrious figures—trainer-drivers, breeders, owners and executives—had been installed, including persons like George Morton Levy, the visionary who brought night racing to New York City (and consequently the nation); Lawrence B. Sheppard, founder of the internationally famous Hanover Shoe Farms; and elite horsemen like Frank Ervin, William Haughton, Delvin Miller, Stanley Dancer and Joe O'Brien.

In 1975, when seven-time North American dash-winning champion Herve Filion was elected to the Fame Hall, a number of eyebrows had been lifted over the fact that the writers had seen fit to usher him through the hallowed doors before Robert Farrington. Farrington, of course, had performed similar driving feats a decade earlier, but was still on the outside looking in when Rambling Willie came along to refresh the scribes' memories. The oversight was corrected with the vote in 1979.

Farrington, Canadian horseman John Chapman, and breeder-owner-executive Max Hempt entered at the same time, with statuettes of them to be lodged in a wing of the Hall of Fame of the Trotter in Goshen, New York. Each was also presented with a specially designed ring that signifies their immense contributions and achievements in the sulky sport. Hardly the jewelry type, Farrington tucked his away in a dresser drawer, plucking it out for only the most special of occasions.

Not that the winter season had been all fun and games. Bob, Vivian, the whole gang, were stunned on January 20 when Paul Seibert, the gentle-natured co-owner of Rambling Willie, suffered a severe heart attack. Seibert had attended a horsemen's banquet the night before and woke with chest pains. Before the day was out, he had collapsed and been rushed to the hospital. Paul, whose heart had withstood any number of cardiac finishes by Willie, was hospitalized for three weeks, then sent home for three months of complete rest. But the Farringtons knew that he was already fudging on his doctor's orders—had been attending the races at Lebanon Raceway near his home in Cincinnati—and took that as a good sign.

Seibert had let them know that he would be sound for the summer ahead if Bob could do the same for Willie.

The job of putting Rambling Willie back together again for the season ahead had been going on for weeks, and it was a blessed relief for Robert Farrington when he could return to that task full-time. It would not bother him at all if his tuxedo sprouted a crop of mold.

The Willie team, with its collective eye on the North American money record, launched the 1979 season on March 18, offering him to Balmoral Park in Chicago as a sort of favor. Bob had always liked Balmoral and knew that it rarely had the opportunity to host the champions of the sport. When it urged him to enter Willie in one of its $9,000 Invitational events—the $4,500 winner's share would put him over the top—he obliged. Chagrin was the order of the day, however, when he was nosed out by an unheralded pacer named Choice Love, leaving him $2,008 shy of the mark.

Even Rambling Willie seemed embarrassed by the upset. A week later at the same track he met essentially the same foes—Choice Love included—and waltzed home a winner by seven lengths. The pugnacious old pacer, seemingly held together by bailing wire, had now earned $1,367,637 in his career, more than any North American harness horse—trotter or pacer—in history! Only the French trotter Bellino II with $1,960,945 and the French trotter Une De Mai with $1,660,627 remained ahead of him, and the conversion of their racing earnings into American dollars made the figures questionable at best.

Then, too, the two foreign horses had been retired, while Willie was still racing, blessed with the opportunity of eating into their plurality of francs with every start if Farrington could keep him racing.

Now sharp and good—for the moment, at least—Willie's boss decided to test him against the big boys (and girls) at The Meadowlands. He ran out of gas in his first Eastern race on March 31, finishing an unfortunate sixth, but bounced back a week later to whip the best pacers in the nation in 1:56 3/5. In his third $30,000 contest in as many weeks, he slogged through mud, parked out most of the way, to win again. He tried the same tough gang—the cast included Dream Maker, Kerry

Gold, Le Baron Rouge and Bonny's Cold Front—in April and wound up a length back in third.

Taking on a field of Invitational pacers in Chicago and tangling with the best in the nation—most of them five and six years younger—at The Meadowlands were two distinctly different propositions, and no one had to explain that to Robert Farrington. Bob, like most horsemen with a *big* horse, kept a probing eye on every one of Willie's prospective opponents—across the nation and up into Canada.

He knew that no horse, even the young and perfectly sound hotshots, could race at The Meadowlands week after week after week, ripping off miles in the 1:56 to 1:54 range, and remain in one piece. His hotshot was hardly young, hardly sound, and he had figured early on that he would pick his shots as the season wore on. When Willie was healthy, he would tackle the toughies for three or four weeks, then head for the hinterlands. After his fourth start at the big track, he loaded his pacer on the van and made tracks.

His first ship was a short one, fifty miles down the New Jersey Turnpike and U.S. Route 9 to Freehold Raceway, still in New Jersey. Bob had always enjoyed Freehold and built up a stock of memories there, both with Willie and other horses. He added to the collection on April 28, winning with Willie in 1:59 over an off track. The winner's cut of the $30,000 R. Bruce Cornell Memorial purse was pleasant and had been collected without undue stress or strain.

Farrington and his fellow traveler were back in Chicago—at Maywood Park—for the next two weeks, notching back-to-back decisions with back-to-back 1:59 2/5 miles. The first was a $25,000 leg of the Maywood Pacing Series, while the latter was the $50,000 final. The cash register continued to jingle with the elderly pacer's deposits.

Three hundred and fifty miles south of Chicago, Willie raced twice at Scioto Downs in Columbus, Ohio, garnering a win and a second. Then it was back to Chicago—this time to Sportsman's Park—and a decision in 1:58 2/5. It was his fifty-fourth score in two minutes or better, with every such mile opening a wider chasm in his all-time lead in that department. Of all the high marks he had set, Farrington was confident his miracle mile total would stand the longest, conceivably forever.

Rambling Willie was holding together, no question about it, and his chief mechanic felt he deserved a chance to test his mettle again in the $321,000 four-leg Driscoll Pacing Series at The Meadowlands. Surprisingly, Willie made an early lead hold up in the first $40,000 leg, winning in 1:57 2/5. But then he could do no better than seventh and fourth in the next two, with both events won by a powerful four-year-old called Abercrombie. Willie raced well in both, pacing in 1:55 2/5 and 1:55 flat, but was no match for Abercrombie's matching 1:54 2/5 performances. Six weeks later, with Glen Garnsey driving as usual, Abercrombie would pace in 1:53—the fastest race mile in harness racing's long tenure as an American sport to that time.

Willie outdid himself in the $171,000 Driscoll final—a race he had won in 1977—traveling in 1:54 4/5, but finishing third to feisty old rivals Dream Maker and Le Baron Rouge. The Farrington entry did manage to outleg four horses in the field, including a soundly beaten Abercrombie.

Abercrombie's skid in the Driscoll finale—he finished seventh—only served to shore up Farrington's original philosophy that no horse was likely to dominate in the fierce competition served up weekly at The Meadowlands.

The big New Jersey track was closing for the season—"And not a moment too early," Bob told Willie's groom, Dean Collins—so the search for temporary homes for the geriatric pacer resumed. There were a spate of invitations—Willie remained a national hero, was wanted by every track—but his trainer was intrigued by a telephone bid from Foxboro Raceway near Boston.

New folks were running Foxboro, had pumped a great deal of cash into modernizing it, and wanted to serve up something that would draw them a crowd. The management scattered suggestion boxes around the plant and urged fans to jot down what they'd like to see most at the rejuvenated track. The top item by far on their "wish-list" was Rambling Willie.

The son of Rambling Fury, meeting New England's best pacers, including Foxboro record-holders Ripping Chief and Fortune Moy, rewarded his Boston area fans with a flashy 1:57 1/5 victory over the five-eighths mile oval. Farrington picked up Willie's $10,000 check, sent his horses and caretaker Dean Collins on to Brandywine Raceway in Wilmington, Delaware, and flew back to Chicago for a day of rest, then a week of driving

Bob Gordon's horses at Sportsman's Park.

Rambling Willie had been racing a normal schedule, lining up behind the starting gate once a week, but that had not been true of his trainer-driver. Bob Gordon, Robert Farrington's close crony who had traditionally trained Willie in California in Farrington's absence, had moved a contingent of his better horses into the Chicago area. Gordon, a native of Ohio like the Farringtons, considered his older friend to be the greatest harness driver in the world, and had pushed and pressed and cajoled until Farrington had agreed to drive them. While the sudden spurt of activity was tiring, Robert F. was obviously enjoying himself in the role of Gordon's designated sulky sitter.

The Farringtons, Bob and Vivian, could ask for no more from life. Rambling Willie was healthy and winning with regularity. Paul Seibert had come all the way back from his heart attack and was again much in evidence when Willie raced. They had moved into their new home at the Mokena farm and it was everything they had expected it to be. And their grandchildren, who lived across the road, were growing into delightful companions, adding a new dimension to their lives.

But on July 25, Inez Ray, Vivian's sister, phoned with the crushing news that the Reverend C. L. Harris had been felled by a massive stroke. Their octogenarian father, one of Bob Farrington's favorite persons, was on the critical list in the Kenton, Ohio, hospital, his speech and all movement on his right side gone, victims of his malfunctioning arteries.

It should not have come as a shock—people of his years were prone to such attacks—yet it was. Reverend Harris, the warm, sprightly, gentle pastor of the church Rambling Willie had supported for so long, had seemed forever durable. To his daughters, to his son-in-law, to everyone who knew him.

He was still a willing, devoted, active volunteer in God's army, preaching His message, presiding at funerals, comforting survivors, braving all brands of Central Ohio weather to call on the sick. He had spent a happy winter accompanying the Farringtons to the banquets honoring Bob, filling his daughter and son-in-law with pride as he, with a firm voice and beaming countenance, offered the invocations to begin the festivities. Typically, he was at work in the J and J Food Market across the street from his home in Rushsylvania—still a part-time employee at age eighty-nine—when the stroke had brought him down.

Inez had warned Vivian to expect the worst, and Vivian's appeals to her Creator were on the modest side during the six-hour drive from Mokena to Kenton. She asked that her father not suffer and that she might see him once more while he lived.

But the Creator was infinitely more charitable than that. The reverend had regained much of his ability to communicate by the time the Farringtons arrived at the small hospital. The right half of his body was still without feeling, the proof of it obvious on his face, but he was talking. Incredibly, he was joking with the nurses who hovered around him.

"I'm having trouble believing this," Inez, as deeply religious as her sister, told Vivian with awe. "You're going to think I'm insane, but Dad was near death when I called you. He really was."

"God does not want Dad yet," Vivian said, believing it.

"Apparently not," Inez agreed.

As days passed, the ravages of the attack receded. All of his verbal powers returned. Gradually the paralysis left his limbs. He was up, walking the corridors of the hospital, providing spiritual comfort to his fellow patients. When he left the hospital, he paid extensive visits to both his daughters, then returned to his home in Rushsylvania. Soon he was presiding at funerals again, but turning the bulk of his pastoral duties over to a younger successor. In early winter, he got in his car and drove alone to St. Petersburg, Florida, where he rented quarters and spent the winter months. "Having a great time," he wrote to his daughters.

Lloyd Harris, like Paul Seibert, had not only been spared, but returned to an existence as full as anyone of their years could reasonably expect. If God was keeping a watchful eye on Rambling Willie . . . if He, indeed, was using Willie as a vessel to spread His word, including the message of tithing, as Vivian Farrington was convinced . . . then it seemed likely that His benevolent umbrella also extended far enough to cover the people closest to the horse.

Divine intervention or no, there surely was something *special* about Rambling Willie—no thinking person could deny *that.* And if the people around him appeared to have nine lives, then Willie himself must have been granted eighteen. With yet another about to be spent.

Bob Farrington had long dreaded the possibility of Willie breaking down in the course of a race, of going so desperately lame that a van had to be sent onto the track to haul the horse back to the barn. He had seen it happen hundreds of times over his long career, and it had sickened him every time. Should such a fate fall to Willie, Bob was convinced the public would charge him with greed, with having raced an unsound horse *until* he fell victim to a crippling injury.

That thought was never far out of his mind, and was with him when he and Vivian flew into Pittsburgh on August 6. The couple rented a car and drove out to The Meadows (not to be confused with The Meadowlands) in nearby Washington, Pennsylvania, where Willie was scheduled to race in a $30,000 Invitational. The Farringtons arrived with light hearts, content that Lloyd Harris was making a remarkable recovery back in Ohio, but the contentment fled Robert Farrington's chest as soon as he began to warm up Willie.

"He's not right," Bob told Willie's groom, Dean Collins.

"Bob, he seemed all right during the week," the worried Collins offered quickly.

"I'm sure he did. And I'm not blaming you," the driver said reassuringly. Farrington knew how conscientious the caretaker was, how sensitive he was. He and Vivian were so taken with the youngster that they not only trusted him alone with Willie on the road, but had invited him into their home when he was back at the farm. Collins occupied a bedroom off the family's handsome "Rambling Willie" room on the bottom floor, where he spent a great deal of his time studying Bob Farrington's winning drives on a videotape playback machine. Dean was a fledgling driver, only then starting his career on the fair tracks, and Vivian had been greatly amused one day when the youngster had jumped up from the machine and shouted, "I've got it! I know what he does! I've learned his secrets."

"You going to scratch him?" Collins asked the man, whose driving secrets he possessed.

"I don't see how I can," Farrington allowed. "He's not really *that* lame, and they built the race around Willie. Spent a lot of money advertising it and everything. Looks like they've drawn a pretty good crowd, and I wouldn't want to disappoint them."

"Maybe he'll warm out of it," Collins offered hopefully.

"Maybe."

In the race, no van was needed to rescue a crippled Willie. He sailed around the track like a speed skater—"I'd never seen his gait any smoother," Vivian Farrington commented later— and had to be smooth and tough to preserve a 1:57 3/5 victory over a tenacious local favorite named Pilot Hill. But heading into the winner's circle, with the race over and the need for gameness past, the gallant gelding was walking on three legs. He was dog lame, so gimpy that Farrington considered calling for a trailer to get him back to the paddock and then on to the barn.

At one point during the overlong ceremonies after the race, Bob reached down, ran his hand up and down Willie's two legs, and confirmed a suspicion that had begun festering in his mind during the short ride to the winner's circle. The injury wasn't in the thick, scarred right leg that had troubled him for years. It was in the left.

"You take him to the spit box," he directed Collins, refer-ring to a closed stall in the paddock where urine samples are taken from horses to assure there were no drugs in their sys-tems when they raced. "I'm going to hunt up a vet."

Dean Collins was still trying to coax Willie into urinating when Farrington returned with Dr. Barry Betts in tow. The veterinarian went directly to Willie's left front leg; Bob had described the problem on the way to the spit box.

"Bow," Dr. Betts said solemnly after his examination. "Bad one."

Farrington nodded. "I thought as much. Can you give him some Bute [Butazolidin, a pain-killer] so we can get him back to the barn?"

Rambling Willie, the richest harness horse in American history, the horse with more two-minute victories than any before him, now had bowed tendons on both front legs. Few trotters or pacers had ever amounted to much after suffering a single bow (and Willie had actually bowed three times on the right leg); hardly a one had ever come back from ruptured tendons on both legs.

The new injury was so bad, the tendon sheath so hot, swollen, mushy and painful, that Willie could not immediately stand the trip back to the Midwest. Dean Collins spent three days tubbing the leg in ice, hosing it and rubbing it, before Farrington felt he could move his horse out of The Meadows.

When he did ship him, he sent him to the Farrington family's homestead farm in Richwood, Ohio. Two veterinarians examined him there, both shaking their heads with pessimism. Then it was on to the stable headquarters in Mokena, where Willie was turned out in his mammoth paddock and another vet was called in. The result was the same. It was doubtful he would ever race again. Farrington had taken his horse to the well once too often.

Willie's "team" accepted the verdict philosophically. Paul Seibert was content to retire the horse. Vivian Farrington, as always, left the decision to God. "If He wants him to race again, he'll race again." Bob Farrington seemed resigned. "He raced four or five years more than I figured, so I guess we should simply be grateful," he said.

Yet, in all their minds, was the ever present knowledge that Willie had been down any number of times in the past, but never counted out. He was tougher than nails, game as a badger, and had the recuperative powers of a horse eight years his junior. As Bob Farrington watched him out in his paddock, chasing flies with his tail, hunting relief from the hot August sun, he wondered whether there might be one more miracle kicking around somewhere for his gimpy champion. At the very least, he decided, he would blister the ailing tendon, the severe-but-effective treatment that had helped the horse to struggle back to the races after the earlier injuries. He fully intended to do that until Bob Gordon intervened.

Gordon spent a great deal of time at the Farrington farm. He thoroughly appreciated the Farringtons' company, gravitating to Bob's bone-dry wit and Vivian's devotion to the spiritual life, which he shared. He also adored Rambling Willie, had considered it a great honor and rare privilege to occasionally train the horse.

Gordon had been wheedling Farrington to send Willie to Dr. Lloyd Salem McKibbin, a Wheatley, Ontario, veterinarian who had been experimenting with laser beams in the treatment of equine injuries. Farrington had been resisting. While he had always been quick to try innovations in the racing game, Willie's trainer could not fathom how a concentrated beam of light might cure a torn tendon sheath.

Bob knew McKibbin, had used him in the past on other horses and had come to respect him. But it wasn't that way with all horsemen, nor with all of McKibbin's veterinary peers. Some considered him a genius; others a grandstander who dealt in the occult.

McKibbin had abandoned the traditional tools and procedures of his profession—blistering, cautery, firing and nerving. Many of the conventional tools of his fellow veterinarians—hypodermic syringes, scalpels and x-rays—played only supporting roles in his operation. He was pioneering and hypeing a phase of veterinary medicine that he felt was more natural, less primitive. McKibbin was into such futuristic procedures as cryo-algia, the freezing of diseased tissue to minus fifty degrees centigrade, and, of course, lasers. But he wasn't above borrowing from the past, either, and he also relied on such ancient treatments as acupuncture and auricular medicine.

While he looked like somebody's placid grandfather, McKibbin was hardly that. He was aggressive, opinionated, and outspoken, all qualities that guaranteed he would be pilloried by his contemporaries and berated by veterinary colleges. But the criticism rolled off his back. "A man has to have criticism," he told one interviewer. "A guy could go right off the deep end if he didn't have someone questioning him from time to time, keeping him on his toes."

Controversial or not, McKibbin had a growing number of horse trainers who were ready to testify that his use of the filtered laser on bowed tendons and suspensory problems had brought their horses back to competitive fitness. Bob Gordon, who had trained horses for McKibbin—McKibbin's own horses and some of his rebounding patients—was one of them.

"What have you got to lose?" Gordon persisted to a stubborn Farrington. "Willie's through anyway. The laser can't hurt him."

"There's always blistering."

"Hah!" Gordon offered derisively.

Then Gordon contrived to have McKibbin phone him at the Farrington farm. He and Willie's trainer were having lunch when the call came. Gordon chatted with the Canadian veterinarian for a while, then told him, "I want you to talk a stubborn jackass into trying the laser on one of his horses." He handed the phone to Farrington.

Farrington and McKibbin talked at length. Bob described Willie's injury. The veterinarian outlined the laser treatment, explaining it caused a horse's body to release an intermediary product that promoted circulation and healing. Like a blister, only gentler, more natural, without pain. Farrington wanted to know if he could use the old-style blister on Willie if the laser program failed.

"Certainly," McKibbin assured him.

"I suppose it might be worth a try, then," Farrington agreed reluctantly.

Rambling Willie left the next day. He spent three weeks at Dr. McKibbin's clinic. Four days before his scheduled return to the Farrington farm, Bob Gordon drove up to train him a mile, to learn whether the treatment had helped. He phoned Farrington, catching him in the Sportsman's Park paddock that night. "Willie's perfect; I trained him in 2:15," he reported.

"Willie never trained in 2:15 when he was dollar sound," his trainer said skeptically.

"He did today," Gordon said flatly.

Rambling Willie returned to Mokena on September 21. Robert Farrington could not believe his eyes. Willie's tendons—both of them—looked tight and tough, cool to the touch. Still disbelieving, positive that he would break down along the way, Bob worked him strenuously over the next two weeks. Then he entered him to race at Chicago's Balmoral Park on October 7. Willie won in 1:59 flat.

Robert Farrington, puttering about the farm the next morning assessing the last few months, felt like a character in a soap opera, or maybe a country-western song—the tides of his life based upon the whims of some unseen writer, fluctuating wildly with the moods of the author.

With more episodes and verses to come.

His wife, he knew, would have no problem identifying the writer.

Chapter 20

*B*obby Gordon, while a dozen years younger, and perfectly at home in the role of protege, had always exerted a mystical kind of influence over Bob Farrington, an influence that Farrington might not have admitted nor even recognized. Gordon's high energy, his talent for squeezing the most out of life, his freewheeling sense of humor, and the fact that he shared Ohio roots, were all part of his appeal to the more reserved Farrington, and it was a rare occasion when he could say no to the younger horseman.

It was Gordon who had persuaded Farrington to try the radical new laser beam treatment on Rambling Willie's tendons, and it was Gordon who had nudged the former driving champion out of semi-retirement and back into the sulky on a more or less regular basis for a portion of the 1979 racing season. Willie, of course, had earned a new, if temporary, lease on life, and Farrington had seemed to enjoy chauffeuring Gordon's horses around the Chicago racing ovals during the summer.

"Tell you what, Chief," the engaging Gordon offered shortly before he and his stable headed back to California for the fall campaign at Hollywood Park. "The first of the year, I'll gather up sixteen or seventeen of my better horses, you round up your six or seven, including Willie, and we'll head for The Meadowlands. Get there early and knock that big Jersey track on its ear. Grab a half-million in purses before those city slickers know what hit 'em."

Farrington squinted over the rim of his cup, took a long

pull at his coffee, and gently set the cup down in its saucer before answering. "Naaah," he said.

"Whataya mean, 'naaah?'"Gordon mimicked. "I'll do most of the training; you do the driving. Show them Johnny-come-latelys, those Herve Filions and John Campbells, how to team a horse. Show 'em what a good 'ol boy from Ohio can do."

"Naaah," Farrington repeated. "I got out of that rat race eight years ago. Jumping in and out of a sulky all night long. Living out of a suitcase. Besides," he added, "I figured I was too old when I gave it all up last time, and I sure haven't got any younger since."

"Baloney!" Gordon scoffed. "Your driving is just as sharp now as it was when you were winning all them national titles back in the '60s. And you can't tell me you didn't have a ball steering my animals this summer, 'cause I could tell by your face that you did."

"Chicago is one thing, The Meadowlands is another," Farrington said defensively. "There's the new house. There's the kids. . . ." He was talking about the large and attractive brick home clearly visible out the window, a home the Farringtons had designed, constructed and decorated until it was a candidate for *House Beautiful* magazine. And he was talking about his grandchildren, Gale Marie, 7, Justin, 6, and Jack Daniel, 2, children of Jim and Karen Farrington Curran. The youngsters lived with their parents across the narrow road leading to the Farrington farm—and the Curran farm, too—and the three had become part and parcel of their grandparents' lives, spending nearly as much time with them as with their parents.

"The house? The kids?" Gordon jeered. "They going to disappear while you're gone? Somebody going to make off with them during the few weeks you're away?"

"Naw," Farrington admitted. "Naw. But there's *her*," he added in sort of half mumble, nodding down at the end of the table, where Vivian Farrington sat stoically viewing the scene. "She'd have a fit, a royal fit."

"Would you, Viv?" the younger man probed, knowing full well that he and his longtime friend had finally arrived at the marrow of the matter.

Vivian Farrington, immaculate as always in a powder-blue

turtleneck and beige slacks, was aware from the outset that the unwanted ball would eventually land in her court. And, like Gordon, knew that it had arrived.

She had listened to the give and take with unsettled emotions. At one time, she had both yearned and prayed that her husband would retire from driving. Or, at least, from *that much* driving. And she had thanked the Lord when Bob had arrived at that decision in 1972. But she had also witnessed the obvious pleasure he had gotten from driving Willie in the years since, quietly basking in the rekindled glow of fame that had come as a result. And 1979 had been an exciting year for Bob—handling Gordon's horses, election to harness racing's Living Hall of Fame, earning the Harness Horsemen International's Man of the Year Award, serving as chairman of the sport's drive for funds in the fight against Multiple Sclerosis—and Vivian understood that it was difficult to slide down from a high like that. Then, too, the accidents that had broken his bones and bruised his body were years in the past, hardly more than dim memories, although all of it, all the rationale, in reality, was academic. The important thing was that Bob wanted it, wanted to resume his driving career in earnest, and had made up his mind some time back. He was merely fishing for her blessing.

"What about it, Viv?" Gordon pressed, fastening a pair of shining and knowing eyes on her.

"Whatever Bob wants," she said softly.

"Bob?"

"I'll think about it," Farrington answered slowly. But then he smiled, and Gordon accurately accepted the grin as unconditional surrender.

"All right!" the younger horseman yelled, slapping the table with the palm of his hand. "Watch out, Big Apple. The Red Man is back in business!"

"I said I'd think about it," Farrington growled.

"Right," Gordon offered with equal severity, then spoiled the effect by adding, "Meadowlands, here we come!"

It was to be another turning point in the life of Robert G. Farrington, a U-turn in a road that had been replete with hairpin curves, close brushes with steep cliffs, engine-straining streaks up lofty mountains, and stomach-wrenching dives into distant valleys. Bob Farrington, a semi-recluse from 1972 to 1979, a man who ventured out of his Mokena, Illinois, lair only to drive Rambling Willie or tour a county fair track with a young and gangly trotter or pacer, was headed back to the big time. Full tilt. Campaigning a twenty-five horse stable at the largest, busiest, richest, gaudiest harness racing track in the world. Driving three, four or even five times a night as he and Bobby Gordon dropped their horses into the entry box and other horsemen prevailed upon him to catch-drive their standardbreds.

It was somewhat like an old quarterback coaxed away from his public relations job and back onto the football field when all the signal callers on his old team were hurt. Like an aging gunfighter shaking off the ravages of time and drink for one more town-saving shootout along Main Street. Like a Muhammad Ali denting the misty mornings to jog off fifty pounds for still another shot at the heavyweight crown.

Bob Farrington loved it. Loved the planning, the preparation, the anticipation. It was dramatic and exhilarating, and soon the entire farm was caught up in it, despite Bob's protests that it was "only temporary, only an experiment." They believed the boss was hellbent to make a comeback and they reveled in it.

Some of the younger farm hands, caretakers like Carol Thompson and Larry Hummel, were still in grade school when Bob had been setting records in the 1960s, but they had read the engravings on the trophies and plaques, wandered through the Farrington scrapbooks, listened to the tales of veteran grooms. They knew the boss had been the main man, the driving king, a decade and a half earlier, and they were convinced he could—and would—climb the ladder again. They were positive the man still possessed the magic, and would not give it up once the public began to applaud his old razzle-dazzle.

The Farrington farm had never been a forlorn place, a lonely place, even in the dead of winter during the years of Bob's sort of self-imposed estrangement from the sport. The boss always had six or eight horses in various stages of training, including the illustrious and sometimes bellicose Rambling Willie, and the farm's indoor equine swimming pool, one of the finest in Illinois, had constantly drawn a number of outside-owned horses, both standardbreds and thoroughbreds.

But the farm, given the best and busiest of times, could not match the excitement and the glamour of the mighty Meadowlands, harness racing's flagship track—its Taj Mahal. It would be cold, sure, racing the winter months in New Jersey, but the accommodations were excellent and there would be no shortage of thrills. Every caretaker at the farm was conferring extra care upon his or her animals, hoping their horses would be good enough to make the Farrington-Gordon traveling team when it headed East.

It was a cold, gray morning in mid-October when all of the hopes, all of the dreams, all of the golden expectations, came crashing down.

The clock read 11:20 A.M. on October 16, 1979, when Vivian Farrington left the barn, bent upon depositing her grandson, Justin, at the school bus stop near his home. The Farringtons' younger grandson, Jack Daniel, was with her, too, due to spend a part of the day at his grandparents' home.

Bob had kissed the younger of the two boys, and sent Justin on his way with a wish that he have a good day. "Study hard," he advised the youngster, hoping, at the same time, that the seven-year-old never got around to asking his grandmother what kind of student his grandfather had been.

"Will you be home for lunch soon?" Vivian asked, glancing back at her husband from the window of the car.

"Should be," Bob promised. "Got one trip left with that New Zealand horse and I'll be done."

"Soup and a sandwich all right?"

"Fine," he said, turning to walk back into the barn and up the long aisleway, where a tall horse named Valiant Dream N stood docilely in cross-ties, waiting to go the last of three training miles that morning. Farrington slid onto the seat of the jog cart while a groom freed the horse from the ties, then fastened the check rein to keep the animal's head up. The pacer ambled slowly out of the far end of the barn and up onto the half-mile training track Farrington had fashioned out of pastureland.

Once up on the track, Bob jogged his horse along until he caught up with Dave Shebroe, a stable caretaker who had been moving along slowly with a Farrington horse called Whoor Chief, waiting for the boss to draw even and offer instructions on the training mile they would go in unison.

"You tuck in behind me and stay tight to my back," Farrington offered as they turned their horses and began to pick up speed for the start of the timed mile. "We'll go down to the half in about fifteen [a minute and fifteen seconds], then let 'em ramble a little at the end of the mile."

"Right, Bob," Shebroe agreed.

Farrington chirped softly to his horse to get him rolling a little faster, then sat back to take in the morning—not that it was much of a morning, he decided. The leaves of the maple trees on the rise to the left had turned, were near their peak of color, but you could not tell it with the pall of grey spread over the land by the thick and dark clouds above. A cool and damp wind hit him in the face as Valiant Dream N came out of the turn and proceeded down the backside of the track.

"He pacing all right, Dave?" Farrington asked, his head swiveling to the rear to inquire of Whoor Chief.

"He's doin' fine, but I'm freezing," the caretaker shouted back.

"Yeah, it's raw. Real raw," Farrington confirmed.

The two horses, beginning to sweat with the effort, moved into the turn at the far end of the egg-shaped oval, negotiated the fairly tight half-circle, and began to pound down the stretch, approaching the point where they had commenced the trip. They would have a half-mile, one more complete tour of the small track, to go when they reached the start.

"When they come out of the next turn, we'll let 'em have their head a little," Bob yelled. "Stay close."

"Gotcha," Shebroe answered.

But they never came out of the next turn. Heading into it, Bob's horse, Valiant Dream N, cross-fired, his left leg reaching over and hitting his right. The left hoof caught on the shoe of the right foot. The hooves were joined for only an instant, but it was enough to trip him, to send him crashing to the earth.

And Shebroe's horse, Whoor Chief, with his nose virtually over Farrington's shoulder, could not avoid the braking, falling Valiant Dream N. In the tangle of two horses and two men, the right hoof of Whoor Chief flew up and struck Farrington in the small of the back even as the veteran horseman was being catapulted out of the jog cart, bound for the turf below. And then the trailing pacer plowed into the tumbling horse and man in front of him.

Dean Collins, Rambling Willie's lanky groom, had been

watching the training session from the end of the Farrington barn, chatting lazily with a couple of fellow caretakers as Farrington and Shebroe circled the track. "Oh, no!" he cried before taking off at a dead run.

First to arrive on the scene, Collins grabbed the halter of one of the horses—he never knew which—and held on until the other two Farrington grooms arrived. They were joined in a moment by a pair of caretakers from the Jim Curran barn across the way. The horses were quickly led away from the prone Farrington so that they would do no more damage.

Collins had grabbed a horse blanket from one of the youngsters on the scene and used it to cover the injured horseman. But Farrington would have none of it. "Get it off, get it off!" he screamed. "I'm burning up!" An astounded Collins immediately removed it.

Farrington's next words sent a shock wave through the already frightened corps of grooms that had assembled around the fallen trainer. "I've broken my back. My back is broken!" he moaned, his voice a blend of pain and terror.

"Don't nobody touch him," Dean Collins commanded loudly. "I'm going to get an ambulance." With that, he sprinted down the slight incline and headed into the long Farrington barn, bound for a telephone in the stable office.

It was Bob Farrington's worst moment ever. He looked up at the sea of faces now staring down at him and recognized no one. The pain was unbearable, but that was hardly the worst of it. He was paralyzed from the waist down. His bladder and bowels had involuntarily failed him, and the degradation of that, along with the horror of paralysis, combined to cloud his mind, to prevent the pain from being even more excruciating. The fractured shoulders and ribs, the shattered leg he had suffered in earlier accidents were superficial wounds in relation to *this* calamity, although it would be hours before he was able to make such a comparison.

Dean Collins' churning legs propelled him down the aisleway of the barn, and he burst into the combination office-lounge fighting for breath. Steve Rosmarin, the Farrington Stable manager-accountant, was on the telephone, talking, ironically, with one of the co-authors of this book.

"Call an ambulance!" Collins gasped. "Bob's hurt bad up on the track."

Without missing a beat, Rosmarin passed the message on to the writer and hung up the phone. In an instant, he had the number and was dialing the Homer Township Fire Department, whose services to the public included a modern emergency vehicle and trained paramedics.

Dean Collins did not wait to describe the accident to Rosmarin. He fled the office, made a sharp right turn, and whipped out through the aluminum door at the front of the barn. He eyed the small collection of cars and pickup trucks parked in front of the building and selected Bob Farrington's pickup. The keys, as he suspected, were in the ignition. With tires spitting dust, he pointed the vehicle toward the Farrington home less than a quarter-mile away.

Vivian Farrington had been in the house less than ten minutes when Collins arrived like a tall tornado. She was arranging flowers in the first floor guestroom; Paul Seibert, her co-owner on Rambling Willie, was arriving soon. Paul had spent a great deal of time with his friends, the Farringtons, since his retirement—most weekends, to be sure—and Vivian wanted the room to be neat and pleasant for his arrival. Heaven knew, Paul, a bachelor, would have the room in mild disarray soon enough, but at least it would be shipshape when he checked in. Jack Daniel Curran, restless and inquisitive like every two-year-old, followed his grandmother from room to room.

"Viv, there's been a bad accident on the track, and we need an ambulance quick!" Collins shouted from the doorway into the vast, two-story Farrington living room. Rambling Willie's caretaker was aware he had already instructed Steve Rosmarin to call the emergency squad, and knew his second appeal made no sense. In retrospect, he realized it was his way of telling Vivian Farrington that her husband had been badly hurt.

Vivian asked no questions for the moment. She went directly to the kitchen phone—where necessary emergency numbers were listed on a small sticker—and punched out the number for the Homer Fire Department. She was told the emergency vehicle had already been summoned and was on its way.

"Who's hurt?" she demanded of Collins as she hung up the phone.

The young caretaker hesitated for a pair of seconds. "Bob," he answered with a half-sob.

"Hurt badly?" Vivian demanded.

"Yes," Collins answered dismally. "His back . . ."

"Come on, Jack Daniel," Mrs. Farrington ordered, grabbing up her small grandson and making for the door.

Vivian and Collins skirted the long barn and drove directly to the scene of the accident. The ride was less than two minutes in duration, but that was enough time for her to compose herself, offer a simple explanation to her grandson, and to appeal for help from the Almighty. Her composure held as she reached her husband although it was strained to the limits. Bob was lying face up in a ditch on the inside of the training track. It required only a glance at his pain-tortured face and the awkward position of his body to gauge the severity of his injuries.

"I've broken my back," he whispered in agony.

"Lie still. Here comes the ambulance."

With that, the emergency vehicle bumped to a stop on the track and three white-clad men poured out of it. The squad had arrived within ten minutes of Rosmarin's initial call—some at the scene said they had made it in five—and the Farringtons would later express their immense gratitude for such swift action.

A chorus of voices warned the medical team that they were dealing with a back injury, adding an extra measure of caution to their careful, professional ministrations. The crowd, now swollen to nearly twenty, looked on somberly—but with growing admiration for the crew—as the medics painstakingly slipped a long board under the ravaged horseman and gently cinched up the straps to keep him immobile.

Vivian Farrington, forgetting nothing, left Jack Daniel in the care of Rhonda Farrington, a niece who worked for the stable, and slipped onto the front seat of the ambulance. The vehicle took off, the driver proceeding slowly over the rough terrain of the farm, then speeding up when he reached the paved road. The two other attendants were in the back with Bob. One was recording his vital signs; the second communicating them to the waiting emergency ward at Silver Cross Hospital, a dozen miles away in Joliet.

The tight control Vivian Farrington had willed upon herself began to unravel en route to the medical center. Bob was moaning and groaning. "Can't you give him something to ease the pain?" she asked sternly of the busy pair in the back.

"I'm sorry, no," one answered calmly. "The doctors will want him alert. Able to tell them where the worst of the injuries are. Once they've diagnosed him, I'm sure they'll give him something."

The short ride to the hospital seemed interminable to Vivian. She'd shared an ambulance with a battered husband before, but none of his wounds had been of this magnitude. Bob, she knew, had a high threshold of pain—or, at least, covered it with a Spartan mask—so his present agony came as a sobering shock to her.

But from start to finish, from the moment that Dean Collins roared into her home urging that she call an ambulance to the conclusion of the long and shattering episode, her faith in God never wavered. It had gotten her and her loved ones through adversities of all description in the past; it would see them through this new cataclysm.

"I can't move my legs. My legs are paralyzed," Bob muttered in panic at one point along the way.

"It's only temporary, Bob. Only temporary," she answered firmly, reassuringly. And knew that it was so.

Bob was wheeled into the emergency ward with the usual cacophony of such a facility swirling around him. Doctors and nurses, alerted that he was on the way, knowing the general nature of his injuries, were ready. They swarmed about his inert frame as he was transported into a waiting room. And Vivian was left alone with her thoughts and her prayers.

The interlude was brief, however. Dave Shebroe and Dean Collins had followed the ambulance in from the farm and came marching into the hospital, two shaggy, grim specters in horse- and farm-ripened clothes. Karen Curran, the Farringtons' doll-like daughter, was not far behind. The telephone began to ring for Vivian about the time she settled herself in a chair in the small hospital lounge off the emergency ward. Steve Rosmarin had been busy alerting Farrington relatives and friends of Bob's latest disaster, and now they were checking in —Aunt Helen Farrington, the Reverend C. L. Harris, Paul Seibert, Vivian's sister, Inez Ray . . .

There was little that Vivian could tell them beyond what Steve had reported in his initial call.

Bob was in Silver Cross Hospital for two hours. X-rays merely confirmed what most had suspected—that he had fractured several of his vertebrae, the bony arches or cylinders through which the spinal cord passes. The condition of the spinal cord itself was not known for the moment.

Complete diagnosis and treatment was beyond the scope of the hospital; Farrington needed specialists and all of the paraphernalia and trappings of a larger institution, one tailored for the delicate handling of spinal cases. He was transferred to one of the best in the world, the Wesley Pavilion of Northwestern Memorial Hospital on the east side of Chicago. His concerned retinue, headed by his wife, followed.

Farrington drew one of the top spinal men in the country, Dr. Paul R. Meyer, Jr., president of the American Spinal Injury Association, and a man with infinite experience in such cases.

It was 11 p.m.—twelve hours after the accident—before Dr. Meyer and his team of assistants were through with their initial examination. Farrington, they said, had broken three vertebrae—one of them so thoroughly that it might be beyond repair—and damaged others. They did not say it to Farrington.

There was a great deal at stake—*everything* at stake—at one point in the long evening when Dr. Meyer asked Bob whether he was able to move his toes. The doctor, who had lived through the same scene hundreds of times, and dreaded it each time more than the last, posed the question calmly, as though he were asking his patient whether he was hungry.

He did not fool Bob Farrington. Farrington, ignoring the pain, tried desperately to wiggle the toes on his right foot. Panic nearly choked him as he failed.

"Try the other side," Meyer directed softly.

Farrington bit his lip, grunted. The toes on the left foot moved. Something more than a sigh emerged from his mouth, something more like the breath you spend trying to extinguish the candles on a birthday cake. It seemed to speak for everyone in the room.

Shortly before midnight, Bob was carted into room 1586 near the end of the hall on the fifteenth floor. He was given a strong painkiller, then permitted to see his wife. When Vivian was out of the room for a moment, the phone rang. It did not occur to Bob Farrington that he should let it ring. He picked it up and found himself talking to a flabbergasted Bobby Gordon.

Gordon, calling from California, had been trying for hours to reach Vivian, or some other member of the Farrington family. Gordon wanted to assure himself that Bob had survived the terrible accident that had been described to him. The victim of the accident gave him that assurance.

In her rush to see Bob, to spend some time with him in his room, Vivian had missed a weary Dr. Paul Meyer. Meyer had gone home, but a nurse got him on the phone for Vivian. The doctor was cautiously optimistic, but warned her it was almost certain her husband would require surgery to fuse the shattered vertebrae. "We'll do it somewhere between ten days and two weeks from now, depending on how quickly some of the damage heals," he said. "But don't you tell him he faces an operation," Meyer added. "Let me break the news when I feel he's able to accept it."

Vivian assured Meyer that she would leave the unwelcome assignment to him.

But the operation was never performed. Never became necessary. Bob Farrington, every bit as tough and resilient as the brilliant old horse he had been campaigning across the country, healed rapidly and well, astounding the hospital's staff. The immediate fear that he might be paralyzed from the waist down quickly gave way to a concern that he might not regain use of his right leg. But that anxiety, too, dissipated as he responded to therapy.

Dismissing surgery, the doctors told Farrington he would be hospitalized eight or ten weeks. But on November 7, three weeks and one day after he had entered Wesley Pavilion, he left the hospital. Walking. Encased in a ponderous brace and leaning on a cane, to be sure, but *walking*!

He was one of the lucky ones, the incredibly lucky ones. Most of the patients who reached the fifteenth floor of Wesley Pavilion, including his roommate, a twenty-three-year-old injured in a motorcycle accident, departed the medical center in a wheel chair. And *never* progressed beyond the chair.

Farrington's recovery seemed to be an outright miracle to everyone but his wife. Oh, Vivian Farrington considered it a miracle, all right, but felt it was a wonderwork with solid foundation. *Prayer*. From the outset, she had asked for prayer from relatives, friends and strangers. And Bob had received cards from all over the nation, cards confirming that people of every creed, color and culture had intervened with the Lord to help Robert Farrington regain the use of his legs. To Vivian, his recovery made complete sense.

Within three weeks, Bob was clomping about the farm, pestering the help, disturbing the routine, an obvious victim of extreme boredom. He discarded the back brace for a time, then planted it in a closet to stay when he discovered he'd gained so much weight that it no longer fit. Eventually, the cane joined the brace in the closet.

As though in sympathy with his boss, Rambling Willie had gone lame again, this time with stifle problems in his rear legs. It was becoming increasingly difficult to keep him sound, with new ailments piling up upon the stubborn old ones. He was trucked back to Dr. Lloyd McKibbin, again with little hope that he would ever step foot on another race track.

The plan for Bob to team up with Bobby Gordon at The Meadowlands for a steady, heady whirl of driving horses had gone up in the air about the time that Farrington was heading for the ground behind the tumbling Valiant Dream N.

The national press had made a great deal of his accident and his brush with permanent disability. The speculation was, in fact, that he would never drive in another race. The great man and his great horse would retire together, it seemed.

Chapter 21

*T*rue, the race had drawn the best pacers fit and ready in the land, and the purse was a respectable $35,000, but those factors hardly added up to the aura of excitement, the near electricity that wafted through the paddock, then drifted up to the well-populated grandstand and clubhouse. It was something you could feel, something almost tangible enough to taste and smell, something that easily transcended the normal Saturday night racing program in early spring at any North American track—The Meadowlands in East Rutherford, New Jersey, included.

The unnatural stir seemed to emanate from the drivers' lounge, radiating from a spot where a rather stocky man was struggling to climb into a one-piece driving suit, a uniform with a pseudo scarlet and silver jacket attached to a pair of white pants. The vinyl jumpsuits were never easy to settle into, and for the man, the chore was even more challenging. He had a tender, sensitive back to contend with and every time he seemed poised to jiggle the suit over his shoulders, another similarly dressed harness driver would arrive to shake his hand.

One by one they came, John Campbell, a twenty-five-year-old who had won 313 races and $3,308,984 in purses in 1979; Buddy Gilmour, a veteran who had recently risen from the ashes of disgrace to reach the near-top again; Herve Filion, whose clowning manner masked the fact that he had netted fifteen national driving titles in recent years; Shelly Goudreau, a career winner of more than $7,000,000; Ron Waples, who had led North America with 443 wins in 1979, as well as a steady parade of lesser lights.

For most, the greeting was brief, the welcome gruff, as though they were embarrassed to say anything that might be construed as sentimental, as being unmanly. "Thought you were dead . . ." they said. "Thought for sure you'd pack it in . . . Can't bear to hang it up, can ya . . . What the hell you doin' here? . . . We don't allow old cripples to race here. . . ."

The man grinned broadly, accepting the rough greetings for what they were, thankful the welcomes had taken that form. "Can't kill miserable old sinners like me . . ." he responded. "Need the money . . . It was either this or pumpin' gas. . . ."

When the man had finally settled into the driving suit and made his way out to the paddock, the press was waiting. More writers and sportscasters and photographers than any track, The Meadowlands among them, could reasonably expect for a non-stakes race on April 5, 1980. The media men and women swarmed around him, sticking microphones in his face, interrupting him while he helped to dress his horse, ordering him here and there for photographs, waiting for him as he came off the track from warming up his pacer.

"How's your health?" they asked.

"Perfect," he fibbed.

"Was there some doubt in your mind whether you'd ever drive again?"

"Not really."

"How come you're driving again?"

"It's what I do for a living."

"Isn't it dangerous for you to drive?"

"No more for me than anyone else."

"What about the horse? Didn't I hear he was finished?"

"You might have."

"But he's all right?"

"Ask him," said the man, nodding over his shoulder.

Eventually they left, most of them. Headed for The Meadowlands' pressbox and its wide assortment of amenities— typewriters, telex, telecopiers, soft chairs, cold cuts, beer. And they were buzzing along the way, more intrigued and inspired by the man's restraint, his understated answers, than had he been loquacious, animated, dramatic.

The rather balmy April evening passed quickly. The first race went to post and resulted in a 1:59 3/5 victory for a pacer named Armbro Blaze N. The second was contested, a 1:57 triumph for an entry called Composite. The third and fourth slipped by. The fifth went to a Bret Hanover son named Happy Touch in 1:58 2/5, and The Meadowlands was right on course for another of those Saturday night programs in which all races went in less than two minutes.

Then it was time for the man's race, the featured sixth. A $35,000 event for Invitational pacers.

The crowd of 23,514 grew quiet, attentive as the first horse in the field popped out of the paddock and began to amble down the track. The tumult in the pressbox skidded to near-silence as the second and third horses appeared on the track. In a moment, all six were there, clomping slowly around the turn for the parade to post.

Ed Gorman, a tall, distinguished-looking gentleman surrounded by a veritable wizard's collection of electronic equipment, cleared his throat, threw a switch, and began to introduce the field over the track's efficient, reach-every-nook-and-cranny public address system.

"Ladies and gentlemen," he said, "these are the horses for the featured sixth race, a $35,000 contest for Invitational pacers at a mile distance. . . .

"Number one is Direct Scooter, owned by the Valiant Racing Stable, George Orlove, Max Fischer and Ruth Fogel. The driver is Warren Cameron. . . .

"The two-horse is Roan Baron, owned by the W.A.R. Stable of Rockwood, Ontario, and driven by Ron Waples. . . .

"Starting from post position three is Battling Brad, the property of the estate of Donald P. Mitchell, Wilmington, Delaware, and handled by William 'Buddy' Gilmour. . . .

"The four-horse is . . ." then a pause . . . "*Ladies and gentlemen, would you please give a warm welcome to two of the toughest campaigners we've ever had here at The Meadowlands . . . Reunited once again after individual injuries that could have ended the careers of both . . . Would you please offer a rousing Meadowlands welcome to the indestructable Rambling Willie and his incomparable trainer-driver, Bob Farrington!*"

The applause started down on the apron, where hundreds jammed against the track fence, and spread up through the stands. It rumbled on like continuous thunder, punctuated only by screams of "Will-eeee! Will-eeee! Will-eeee!"

The man turned to the crowd, a shy smile on his face, and touched the brim of his helmet.

*O*n Saturday night, December 27, 1980, a pacing colt by the name of Niatross sped around the Pompano Park, Florida, harness track in 1:54⅗ to ring down the curtain on a two-season racing career that had left the racing sport, its fans, and its writers slack-jawed.

Niatross was a freak, the writers said. Niatross had skipped a couple of generations in the genetic process, horsemen claimed. The colt had won all thirteen of his races as a two-year-old in 1979, captured all but two of his twenty-six contests at three, chewed up seven major world records and a spate of track marks, won the pacing Triple Crown, reduced the sport's all-time speed record to 1:49⅕ in a time trial, earned a milestone $2,019,213 in purses, and was a runaway winner of Horse of the Year honors both seasons he raced.

His swan song at Pompano, like all his 1980 races, drew media coverage of a quantity and quality that American harness racing had not known since the halcyon days of the immortal Dan Patch—when the horse was king and the automobile little more than a gleam in Henry Ford's eye. Before the December weekend was out, Niatross' two-season blitzkrieg of the record book would be recycled and recounted by almost every newspaper in the land. And his picture-perfect frame, fresh and unblemished legs, and handsome, noble head would be showcased by two of the nation's three major television networks which had been on the horse's bandwagon for some time and wanted to share in the lemming-like eulogy.

Niatross' last dance, waltzed amid the pink and white splendor of Pompano Park, clearly overshadowed a harness racing happening occurring some 1,300 miles north of Florida's glittering Gold Coast. Hours earlier on the same day—December 27—with temperatures eventually climbing to twenty-six degrees, a scarred, grizzled, creaking pacer had toured the Maywood Park, Chicago, half-mile oval in 2:01 to seal a narrow triumph in a $15,000 contest called the Billy Direct Handicap.

The horse, of course, was Rambling Willie, and it was his sixth win in a row. Of far more significance, it was the one hundredth win of his protracted and turbulent career. And researchers were still wading through the sport's history to discover the last American standardbred to turn that tenacious trick when this was being written.

From the night that Bob Farrington and Willie had commenced their joint and sentimental comeback at The Meadowlands in April to the instant his steam-churning nostrils reached the wire at Maywood, the venerable pacer had gone to post thirty-three times in 1980. And the ten-year-old Willie, whose every race could have been his last, had won fifteen of those matches, adding still another $196,398 to his astonishing collection of lifetime earnings.

In truth—and for a change—1980 had been a relatively uneventful year for Willie and his ever-loving team. The old horse had not only raced well, but gone the distance with more than a mere semblance of soundness. Bob Farrington had recovered from his fractured back—"Well, ninety percent, at least"—and driven in 110 races. Vivian Farrington was still tithing to the West Mansfield, Ohio, Church, but sending a portion of Willie's paychecks to other religious charities since her father was no longer pastor. The Reverend C. L. Harris had come most of the way back from his 1979 stroke, preached an occasional sermon in central Ohio churches and was still in demand for weddings and funerals. Paul Seibert was in good health, certainly well enough to follow his favorite horse from track to track. Dean Collins continued as Rambling Willie's yeomanly caretaker, while Aunt Helen Farrington never wavered from her duty as the Farrington family's faithful historian. Only one jarring note disturbed the year's equilibrium; Karen and Jim Curran, the Farringtons' daughter and son-in-law, ended their marriage, saddening everyone around them.

But that was 1980, ancient history. Now it's 1981, with a new year, a new chapter poised to unfold. Of course, the Farringtons' horse is no longer the richest in American history;

his $1,800,705 is now second to the $2,019,213 collected by the over-achieving Niatross. But, then, Niatross is retired, about to begin stallion service at Castleton Farm in Lexington. And Rambling Willie? Well, Willie is in to race Saturday night at Maywood Park.

Donald P. Evans
Philip S. Pikelny
Columbus, Ohio
February 3, 1981